Quilty as Charged

Quilty as Charged

UNDERCOVER IN A MATERIAL WORLD

by spike gillespie

UNIVERSITY OF TEXAS PRESS, *austin*

Requests for permission to reproduce material
from this work should be sent to:
Permissions
University of Texas Press
P.O. Box 7819
Austin, TX 78713-7819
www.utexas.edu/utpress/about/bpermission.html

♾ The paper used in this book meets the
minimum requirements of ANSI/NISO Z39.48-1992 (R1997)
(Permanence of Paper).

LIBRARY OF CONGRESS CATALOGING-IN-PUBLICATION DATA

Gillespie, Spike.
    Quilty as charged : undercover in a material world / by Spike
Gillespie. — 1st ed.
        p.   cm.
    ISBN 978-0-292-70599-9 (cl. : alk. paper)
    1. Quilting. 2. Quiltmakers. 3. Patchwork quilts. I. Title
    TT835.G3324   2007
    746.46'041—dc22   2007012952

With love and gratitude to

----

my mother, *Dolores Gillespie*, who sewed my clothes when I was little,
who could turn sheets into curtains and create elaborate costumes
out of thin air, and who made me the most beautiful prom dress (even
though I really didn't want to go to the prom) for sixteen dollars

■

Theresa May, for understanding what I want from my writing life,
for knowing exactly what sewing is all about, for teaching me to see
where these two things—and everything, for that matter—merge
in this big, crazy world, and for insisting I order lunch
and dessert (oh, those ironic "cannoli")

■

Norma Bradley Allen, for sharing not only her quilting tales
but also her vast wisdom, brilliant advice, and constant support

■

and to
Sarah Woelk, who dreamed this whole project up in the first place,
who took me to my first (and second and third) IQF, who has been
a financial and emotional and fabric patron, and who guided me
through my first attempt at quiltmaking

■

Contents

Color section follows page 14

Acknowledgments

First and foremost, thanks to Theresa May, for taking a chance on me, not once but twice, and publishing two of my books. And thanks to Mike Tolleson, for helping me with the legal stuff. Thanks to all the quilters who participated—too many to name here, but I do want to mention Arlene Blackburn, Lut De Meulder, Debbie Sylvester, Hollis Chatelain, Debbie Armstrong, Elise Judy, Hella Wagner, Inge Mardal, Steen Hougs, Jote Khalsa, Laura Freeman, Stacy Michell, Marti Michell, and everyone from the Austin Area Quilt Guild who took the time to answer my survey, and all the other quilters who answered my survey.

Also thanks to Henry Mowgli Gillespie, Ross Harper, Max Tolleson & Jo Ann Schatz, Paula Judy, Claudia & Mike, Jason & Luisa, Christopher McDougall, Jill & Kenan, Kat & Richard, Chris, Everett, Ann & Hilary Johns, Eli Durst & Emma Woelk, Diane Fleming, Erin & Steve & Wilson, Paul Klemperer, Hank Stuever, Dean Robinson, Sue Neal, Anna Borne, Adam & Caroline Wilson, my Griffin School peers and students, George III & Brian & Cecil & Cooper, Southpaw Jones, Molly Ivins, Betsy Moon, the booksellers at BookPeople, everyone at BookWoman, my dealers at Hill Country Weavers, Riki Dunn, Norma Bradley Allen, and Shaun Jordan for gifting me with his grandmother's quilts.

A really, really huge thank-you goes to Karey Bresenhan and Bob Ruggiero for putting up with me and my constant questions for all these years.

An unspeakable debt of gratitude goes to Herman Bennett, with whom I spend each night beneath the quilts. And with thanks to Satch, Tatum, and my darling Princess Bubbles, for all the support and for making room for Herman.

Introduction

If there existed a book titled *Women Who Quilt and the Men Who (Are Forced to) Let Them*, the tome would be filled with the sheepish testimony of countless Fabric Widowers. Here, these otherwise strong and domineering men would confess their powerlessness over wives who've been infected with what the quilting community terms "quiltpox." Put conservatively, when it comes to their art, quilters are enthusiastic to the point of rabid fanaticism (a line most would gladly cross were they not held back by life's constraints: work, chores, kids, husbands, and the sad fact that sooner or later, no matter how badly you want to finish a quilt, you have to stop and sleep once in a while).

According to the latest industry statistics, twenty-one million Americans are currently working on quilts. This is a broad-stroke number—"working on" could be defined as merely possessing a quilt magazine with the hopeful but delusional intent of reproducing a quilt pictured therein "one of these days." Or it could refer to having a project half-done and sitting in the basket by the sewing machine for the past five years waiting (perhaps in vain) to be completed.

But for more than one million of the twenty-one million, a subset known as Dedicated Quilters (DQs), "working on" means going at it with a vengeance—maybe cranking out a dozen quilts in a year, maybe spending three years creating a single quilt that will win Best of Show at one of the big annual shows. But always—regardless of pace, regardless of technique (hand or machine sewn, pieced or whole cloth), regardless of style (bold and contemporary or calm and traditional)—for this group, "working on" means performing some quilt-related activity nearly every day.

These women (99 percent of all quilters are women) spend over $500 per year on quilt-related purchases. With an average annual income of $75,000, many of them happily spend much more than that. In 2000, DQs forked over $1.7 *billion* (an 83 percent increase over the 1997 figure.)

In 2004, at the International Quilt Festival (IQF)—the largest annual gathering of quilters in the world—over fifty-four thousand attendees from across the globe poured into George R. Brown Convention Center in Houston. Gawking and walking, they took in more than 1,900 displayed quilts, snapped up fat quarters to heap upon already towering fabric stashes back home, and reveled in a glut of round-the-clock quilt talk with other elated stitchers.

IQF's producers have been successful enough to add a new annual spring show. They also put on an international show once every other year. Additionally, there are a number of other major quilt shows, including the Pacific International Quilt Festival and the American Quilter's Society Quilt Show and Contest, held annually in Paducah, Kentucky. Internationally—for quilting has caught on at a frenzied pace in the UK, Japan, and Australia—there are still more shows, such as the annual festival in Yokohama, Japan, each November and the Quilts UK Show in Malvern, England, in the spring.

At these big shows, the stakes are incredibly high. At Houston's IQF 2004, nearly $70,000 in prizes was awarded, with $10,000 going to Best of Show winner. Paducah show purses have weighed in at over $100,000. The competition is fierce and jaw-dropping, dramatically illustrating how what was once an art of resourcefulness—recycling old clothes and rags and flour sacks into patched-together blankets—has turned into an art of the finest form: We're not talking bedspreads; we're talking museum-quality work that sells for tens upon tens of thousands of dollars.

Beyond the flashy shows there are the little shows. Held in public libraries, churches, small museums, state fairs, and other smaller venues all over the United States, they offer hundreds of opportunities for quilters of varying skill levels to demonstrate their passion and offer the viewing public—many of whom are unfamiliar with the intricacies of quilting—a close-up view of the hard work, microscopic details, and tremendous time commitment quilts require. This is also a place for newcomers and quilting hopefuls to whet their appetites—"quiltpox" is quite contagious in such a setting.

My own passion for quilting was sparked by an article I wrote on the topic, suggested by my friend Sarah, which appeared in the *Dallas Morning News* in January 2002. I confess having one goal when I set out to write that story: pay the rent. I had no idea I was about to cross a threshold into an alternate, fabric-filled universe that would wrap me in its batting and not let me go.

Prior to that article, my only knowledge—if you can even call it that—of quilts was this: for years I'd slept beneath a store-bought quilt, which I never gave much thought beyond two facts—I liked the way the cotton felt, and I liked how just being in the same room with a quilt brought me immediate comfort.

The comfort I derived from that quilt didn't date back to any particular real-life memories, say, me sipping hot chocolate and reading *Little Women* in a nookish window seat, huddled beneath a well-worn quilt made by my great grandmother. As far as I know, no one in my family made quilts. But somewhere along the line, the idea of quilts equaling all things good and warm and right was implanted in my mind. Too, my love of quilts no doubt was an extension of my love of blankets, which I'm certain was born of the nomadic life I lived from eighteen through twenty-eight. I might have to leave furniture, books, and friends behind as I moved (and moved again, and again, forever restless). But blankets could always be folded up and smooshed into some crevice in the car, to be brought along to whatever new destination I landed in, ready to lay the foundation for coziness I liked to establish as soon as possible in a new place.

When that quilt wore out, I put it in the mudroom for my beloved dogs, Satch, Tatum, and Bubbles, because even though the thing was ragged, it still emanated a sense of comfort (the dogs agreed). Not long after, I replaced it with another, fancier, thicker quilt, also a department store purchase. By then I was aware of sweatshops and knew the quaint description "imported," which appeared on the package, was merely a nice euphemism to cover up the working conditions of the women who were forced to make quilts for, I'm guessing, pennies per day of constant sewing in unpleasant working conditions.

But I silenced the guilty voice in my head. Not in my wildest dreams did it occur to me I could learn to quilt. Quilting involved sewing. I did not sew. I'd sooner tape, staple, safety-pin together, or simply throw away torn clothes.

Under no circumstances would I voluntarily undertake a from-scratch sewing project.

■

Researching the quilt story for the *Dallas Morning News* was quite an adventure. I fast discovered that dedicated quilters belong to a large, not-so-secret club with members all around the world. I also learned that if you call one quilter for quotes, you will immediately be given the names of at least a half dozen other quilters to interview. At some point I was forced to stop my interviews—not because I'd heard enough to satisfy me, but because the space allotted my story was extremely limited.

In the final edited version, the one that appeared in print, my editor insisted on cutting back my quotes from quilters and replacing this information with quite a bit about store-bought quilts. Her reasoning was that many women reading the article would want quilts but would have no interest in making them. Lut De Meulder, one of the quilters I interviewed for that story who has since become a great friend of mine, wasted no time getting on my case when the piece ran. How *dare* I give so much space to sweatshop quilts? she demanded.

At the time, while I did clearly recognize the great difference between homemade and store-bought quilts, I didn't quite realize my "crime" in lumping the two together as I had. Although I apologized to Lut, I also defended myself—I didn't have much of a choice in the matter, I told her. And it was true—I was forever deferring to editors in my newspaper work, and this case was no different. If the piece was going to run at all, I had to accept my editor's insistence that I discuss shopping for quilts as well as sewing them.

Rather than hold a grudge, Lut did something quite admirable. She befriended me, and over the years, she took (and still takes) the time to educate me. For my birthdays she's given me quilting books and fat quarters. Thanks in great part to her efforts, I'm finally quilt-wise to the point that if I could go back in time, I'd certainly argue with my editor that the two types of quilts should never be lumped together again.

But full-blown quilt fever did not seize me overnight. Besides Lut's efforts, I was also being nudged by Sarah. Since writing my article, it had finally dawned on me that Sarah's collection of quilts was the perfect blend of form and function. Prior to my article I was vaguely aware that her house was full of dogs and kids, each on a couch under a quilt, but I'd never scrutinized her work before, hadn't even really realized the quilts were carefully designed. Now I looked and

I saw, and I was increasingly excited with each new discovery I made. These were not haphazard, thrown-together productions. They had specific patterns, fantastic color schemes, and special touches—embroidered cartoon characters and mementos of big family events. It still didn't enter my mind that I might be able to do this art, but my appreciation for quilts was growing keener.

In the fall of 2002, Sarah and I were both reading a book called *Word Freak*, by Stefan Fatsis, in which the author shone his journalistic light upon the wacky world of Scrabble fanatics. I'm not talking about friendly family rounds of the word game that get a little out of hand. I mean competitive Scrabble players who dedicate large parts of their lives to improving their skills and who enter tournaments to win big bucks. In addition, Fatsis decided he, too, would work toward the goal of becoming a Scrabble champ.

Word Freak is a great book, inspirational on more than one level. Over the course of reading it, Sarah, both a quilter and a woman prone to many brilliant light bulb moments (not to mention an excellent Scrabble player), came to me and announced, "We need a book like this about the quilting world. And you need to write it."

I immediately fell in love with this idea. If Sarah believed that I *could* quilt, then maybe I could quilt! And how wonderful that my most important qualification as perfect-author-for-the-job was my near-complete lack of knowledge on my topic. Whereas most books are best written by experts, in this case my blank slate would be a boon. I could keep a running account of how I went from hopeless fumble-fingers to quilting genius. Being a romantic and, too often, an idealist, I envisioned immersing myself into a fascinating subculture and emerging later as a card-carrying member, adored by my peers for my matchless quilting skills.

Well, it's been a couple of years since that vision of mastering the art of quilting first visited me. I won't tell you here what level of success I've had (or not)—you can read on and follow my sewing (mis)adventures in detail. But you've probably noticed, if you're a dedicated quilter, that my work has yet to appear on the cover (or any other pages) of well-known (or even unknown) quilting magazines. And if I were you, I wouldn't stand in front of the Best of Show slot holding your breath, looking for my name to appear with the winning quilt anytime soon.

Nonetheless, I certainly have had (and am still having) a lot of fun exploring the quilting world. I've met more than a few enthusiastic quilters, some famous, some not. I've conducted a survey that netted me piles of great responses. I've attended three International Quilt Festivals (so far). And I've found that, no matter where I am, if I bring up quilting in conversation, there's always someone within ten feet who is either a quilter or knows a quilter or has a story to tell of a favorite quilt.

My goal with this book, besides recounting my own personal quilting adventures, has been to capture and share just a few of the great stories I discovered along the way. My regret is that there is no way I could possibly present all the stories I uncovered. Maybe I need to write a series—because certainly there is more than enough material (pun most certainly intended) out there to fill volumes.

Before I commence to detailed sharing of these quilting stories, I want to take a moment to recall a great conversation I had at the outset of writing this book. I'd already written a proposal, over fifty pages, which I submitted to my then agent. Not a quilter, this woman didn't get what I was aiming for. At first she asked if I might instead prefer to write a book about knitting. Mind you, I am an avid knitter, much better at that craft than I am at sewing. But the way this woman put it, it was as if she thought the two were interchangeable.

When I made it clear to her that quilting was unique and that I intended to stick to the topic, she acquiesced and ceased with her call for me to write a yarn about yarn. Still, while she reluctantly agreed that quilting might work as a topic, she didn't share my vision for project execution. I wanted to write about living, breathing quilters—traditionalists, contemporary artists, hand quilters, machine quilters, etc.—patching together an eclectic bunch of profiles. She suggested that instead I write a book about the history of quilting.

I admit I understood her motive for this suggestion—the book market these days is most often looking for a formulaic, surefire best seller. Pitching a wacky people collage, as I had, didn't meet that goal. But with all due respect to my agent's needs and visions and the demands of the publishing market, not only did I feel like the history of quilting had been adequately covered numerous times by people far more knowledgeable than I, but it also didn't come close to what I wanted to accomplish.

So I parted ways with that agent, next approaching the agent who had sold *Word Freak*, since that was my inspiration. He read my proposal and did get it but wanted me to reshape my idea to follow the lives of just a few quilters, their ups and downs, the arcs of their stories—very beginning, middle, and triumphant ending. Not a bad idea, but again, not my vision.

Which is when I made the very good choice to query Theresa May, who had edited a previous essay collection of mine. Would UT Press ever even be interested in the topic of quilting, written in the spirit of quiltmaking—that is, many small stories pieced together?

Theresa invited me to drop off my proposal. Within twenty-four hours, she called to set up a lunch date: Yes, she wanted the book. Besides the very good feeling that comes whenever a book idea gets a green light, I got something else from Theresa. I knew she was a seamstress—she makes amazing costumes for theater productions.

During our lunch we talked at length about sewing. I confessed my near phobia of the activity while she expressed her joy in it. I didn't need to work to convince her that capturing many small tales of everyday quilters would be exciting. She already understood that passionate sewers hear the hum of a busy sewing machine the way orchestra patrons hear the sweet triumph of a masterfully performed symphony presentation.

Theresa was the one who pointed out to me what a perfect metaphor quilting is for women's lives. We all have our stash—of skills, memories, drawbacks, drama, tragedy, and joy. And from this stash we piece together our lives, each of us creating an amazing and unique pattern. This resonated deeply.

And so with the encouragement of Sarah and Lut and Theresa, I set out to piece together my first quilt and to piece together this tale of many quilters. While I certainly encountered many obstacles along the way, from broken needles to a tape recorder that chose to malfunction at a crucial moment, I have come away much richer for my experiences.

The Mysteries of Quilting Revealed

- -

Everything starts at the seam.

—TIM DELAUGHTER, THE POLYPHONIC SPREE

1

Quilt Show Virgin

Sarah picks me up in her station wagon, and I climb in the backseat. Next stop, Kathy's house. Kathy throws her luggage in the far back and then takes her place up front, next to Sarah. Sarah aims the car southeast on Highway 71, leading us from Austin to Houston. Destination: International Quilt Fest 2002, the twenty-eighth gathering of the largest quilt festival in the world. My cohorts' rapid-fire dialogue, filled with quilting terms and information new and strange to me, often goes right over my head. I sit listening, trying to absorb just a little.

This road trip is a fitting metaphor—me in back like the child with so much to learn, those two up front like my wiser parental units, avid quilters eons beyond me and my paltry quilting knowledge. Though they see each other much less often than they did back when their kids attended the same elementary school years ago, Kathy and Sarah make a point of meeting once a year to attend IQF together.

Me? I'm a Quilt Show Virgin. No matter how well they explain in advance, nothing they say will keep me from nearly falling over when I first walk in the door of the ship shaped George R. Brown Convention Center. Displayed throughout the 500,000-square-foot facility are sixteen hundred quilts selected to be in the show, another God-knows-how-many being offered for sale in the eighty bazillion vendor booths, plus hundreds of sewing machines, thousands of spools of thread, all manner of quilting tools and gadgets and patterns and videos. And, of course, there are the quilters.

I am so immediately overstimulated I'm not sure where to begin: quilt watching or people watching? Sarah and Kathy have an established routine. They quickly abandon both me and each other, marking this departure with the agreement that all three of us will reconvene at the Best of Show quilt at 1:30 for lunch. Until then, it's every woman for herself, good luck and godspeed.

I am genuinely awestruck—at the overabundance of overabundance on all counts. The enthusiasm here buzzes palpably, the quantity of quilts a vast sea of patterns and colors, some traditional, some anything but. I take an escalator to the second level and walk over to an enormous porthole where I can look down and get an overview. This perch offers a different perspective, yes, but hardly one less daunting. Though everything looks smaller, I can see all of it at once, and this big-picture effect is dizzying. I try to strategize a plan of attack. I will go back down there, start on the first aisle, and work my way up and down each aisle methodically.

No, I won't. Because I will be continually distracted, eye caught by one quilt or another, feet unable to resist the urge to follow. I'm not alone in feeling lost and overwhelmed. I hear one woman on a cell phone instruct the party on the other end—someone here in this building with us—"Give me your coordinates. I can't find you."

Taking in the finalists and award winners for the Husqvarna Viking Gallery of Quilt Art's competition, Masterpieces: A Voyage of Self-Discovery, I listen as a skeptical attendee moves in close to an "art" quilt, with uneven edges and unorthodox technique quite visible.

"This is Wonder Under. This is not stitched," she complains, pointing at the fabric. Then, noting the hefty price tag, she adds, "For three thousand dollars, I want it stitched!"

Her friend chimes in, "This one is five thousand. I didn't know we could sell quilts for that much."

With a knowing nod the first woman informs her, "They do, child."

Of course, I have no idea what the hell Wonder Under is, though I use my context clues to guess it's probably some sort of glue. And so my morning progresses—I stumble through the displays in a happy trance, eavesdropping, trying to guess what people are talking about, trying to decide what I like and what I don't. Quilting terms float around my head, unrecognizable to my ears, reminding me of a trip I took to Japan when I did not speak a word of Japanese.

Criteria for excellence elude me. Thus far no one has shown me what to look for, like tiny, even hand stitches on the backside of a quilt or why this or that technique has pleased the judges. I'm just moving from quilt to quilt, mouth agape. Even the ugly stuff doesn't bother me—I pause and scrutinize all.

At some point, I come upon a quilt that features a picture. Whereas some traditional quilts stick with tried and true patterns, classic blocks of patches, or even whole front pieces quilted to whole back pieces (for the purpose of showing off spectacular, elaborate stitching), others feature picture images that are nearly photographic. In this case, a sensation overcomes me as I look at a quilt depicting a river running over rocks.

I look at the placard and nearly start to cry. Goosebumps rise on my arms. No wonder it looks familiar—this is the Chimneys, a particularly grueling hiking trek in the Great Smoky Mountain National Park that I tackled more than

I was living in Weybridge, Surrey, in England, and a friend wanted to take a quilting course but didn't want to go by herself. I had been doing home sewing for decades but had never made a quilt. So I joined her in the class in a neighborhood city center, and as it's said, "The rest is history." I was hooked and have been quilting ever since—yes, even to the exclusion of the home sewing! My friend never completed her first sampler quilt, which was the class project.

I've been asked many times to make a quilt for someone for money, but I never have, because I think the leisure and joy of quilting would become like work. And I don't want that!

At present, I am living in Paris, France—where patchwork is alive and well, and I belong to a small quilt group and to the France Patchwork Association. Quilting has been an excellent tool for introducing myself to others in a new environment. I like to mention in small groups that I'm a quilter and wait for the response. I've added a few new members to the French quilt group this way. And I meet and share with other quilters each month from Germany, Canada, England, France, and of course, many U.S. states, including Texas, Florida, and California. The friendships will last, just like the quilts. —Rita Loyd, Paris, France

once when I lived in Tennessee. Granted it's not Michelangelo's *David*, but still, I am pulled toward it, breathless, and tears spring to my eyes. Later, I'll learn that this picture was not pieced together from bits of fabric—at the time I just figured all quilts were created as such. In fact digital photos of the actual river were printed on the fabric, which was then quilted.

Though I don't have enough insight yet to form an opinion on the use of such a technique, when I discover this information for a moment I'm a little let down. But then I let that go and tell myself that if the quilt moved me, it moved me, and that is enough.

Lunchtime comes too fast. I catch up with Sarah and Kathy in front of *Flowers of the Crown*, 2002's Best of Show, quilted over a period of three years by Shirley Kelly of Colden, New York. Though based on a photo, this picture *is* pieced together, and I'm flabbergasted at the impossibility of the minute details. A quilt guardian, wearing white cotton Mickey Mouse gloves, turns up a corner, and we all lurch forward for a look at the back. I laugh to myself, imagining this display as the equivalent of a topless bar for women. As with strip joints, everyone here would love to touch the goods, but everyone also knows that doing so is strictly verboten.

We adjourn the show floor for lunch; then it's back down to the floor, where Kathy disappears and Sarah and I return to *Flowers of the Crown*. We're lucky because the perky Shirley Kelly, creator of this quilt and winner of the show, is now present, discussing her art.

She explains how she's gotten her husband to take her quilting seriously over the years. "He knows that I'll buy him a goody when I get home after I win a quilt contest," she beams. "One year I bought him a tractor." The audience laughs its approval, and Shirley adds, "Plus, now he knows I'm a legitimate working woman. Half-hour dinners? No problem!" The crowd applauds wildly.

We exit the big ship *Quilty-pop* around suppertime and head over to our hotel to collect ourselves. Sarah has rented us a room at the Four Seasons, the choice place for festivalgoers to stay. It's a tricky business getting a room here, and money alone does not talk loud enough to secure one. The hotel allots only a certain block of rooms for quilters. To procure one, you have to call in at 7 a.m. on New Year's Day, eleven months in advance of the festival. Otherwise it's hello Hyatt or some lesser hotel further out. The fancy appointments of the Four Seasons make it most desirable, as does the location—the place is a two-minute walk from the convention center.

After unburdening ourselves of the day's purchases, we head back out in search of legitimate food. The effort proves futile, as everything nearby is packed with big hungry quilters. Giving up on finding any place with less than an hour wait, we come up with a delightful Plan B. Back in the room, we order room service. Kathy and Sarah spread their new supplies across a queen-size bed, compare notes, and work on continuing my limited education. I get a whiff of myself fresh from a verbena-soap hot shower—such a relief to my aching legs upon which I stood for eight hours with no more than a thirty-minute break. While they continue to talk about all their great finds, I collapse into a deep hard sleep, only to get up and do it all again.

Because, as an artist and single mother, I am perpetually broke, and furthermore, because I really wouldn't know what to buy to get started as a quilter, I manage not to purchase anything through all of Day One and most of Day Two. I tell myself I'm on a fact-finding mission. I tell myself not to be materialistic. (Aside. Please note that from here on out I will stop making asides every time I use a word like materialistic or cover or any other sewing pun. Please also know that even though I'm not noting it, I am giggling to myself because, if you haven't guessed from the title of this tome, I am a major sucker for all puns, good and, perhaps especially, bad.)

But I break down at the end of Day Two. I can't help myself. I buy Sarah a beautiful piece of silk, not because I think she'll like it but because, frankly, I covet it but can't justify buying it for myself. This way at least I'll get to look at it. I also buy a long, thin neon acrylic ruler. I am utterly clueless as to its purpose and am far too embarrassed at the booth to ask. I feign confidence—Ah! Just the thing I was looking for!!—as I pay for it. Likewise, I whip out the false confidence to pick out a bit of fabric. I am unclear on how much I'll need, but I buy what I like and imagine the beautiful quilt I'll make.

Sarah and Kathy laugh when they see my bright ruler, holding it up, trying to determine what its purpose might be. They explain this thing is certainly not a basic tool, though they do grant me that it is a pretty color, if you're into electric acid green. They're less hopeful about my fabric choice. Having no knowledge, I did not choose quilting cotton; I chose soft flannel, which they tell me can be hard to work with. I try not to be embarrassed at my first haphazard choices, made from love, not knowledge. Even if the fabric is a bad choice for a first quilt, I still love the way it feels, and I can't resist reaching in the bag numerous times on the drive home to rub it between my fingers.

2

Sew What?!

Prior to November 2002, the last time I sewed was in a mandatory home-ec situation in eighth grade back in 1977, when my failure to sail through a Jiffy pattern wrap-around skirt project brought tears of deep pain and bitter disappointment to the rims of the eyes of my sewing teacher, she of the apt Dickensian title, Mrs. Haggard. My time in Mrs. Haggard's sewing portion of this two-component course—cooking was taught in another wing by a much younger, much perkier teacher who gushed about the Beatles and taught us cheesecake recipes to break men's hearts—doubled as an inadvertent DNA study. I proved that sewing is not, in fact, genetic.

My mother was a marvelous seamstress. With nine kids and no budget, she had to be. She was astonishingly resourceful—snapping up ends of bolts and oddly patterned material, deeply discounted because nobody else would be caught dead in, say, denim pants with wide blue and white vertical stripes. I well remember my kindergarten dress—blue background with yellow and green houses printed on it, a white collar, a solid burnt orange tie down the front. I loved it. And my prom dress—created first stitch to last for sixteen dollars, swanky heart-shaped faux mother-of-pearl buttons included.

Me? I was horrible with a sewing machine, instantly frustrated, resistant to learning. Perhaps the machine symbolized for me the road to disdainful house-wifery, a goal my father named for me, holding it up like some threat when I mentioned wanting to go to college instead. Which isn't to say that I dismissed running a house as something done by lesser beings. My mother's ceaseless talents—child rearing, budget stretching, cooking for a family of eleven—inspired awe, not condemnation. But I always banged heads with my father—even if being a wife had, in fact, come with a $200,000 per year salary (ha!), I would've rejected the role out of hand, another way to rebel against his plans for me.

Most likely my contempt of sewing was more of the moment, a result of the disappointment I felt at my immediate failure, my abject lack of coordination (you expect me to work with my hands and a foot at the same time *and* keep my seams straight?), and the fact that there were no boys in the class with whom I might flirt and distract myself from the harsh and critical stare of my teacher bearing down on me each time I wrecked my wrap-around-skirt project anew.

I quickly and gladly put sewing behind me after eighth grade, save for the occasional button reattached or patch affixed. And then, twenty-five years later, during my second day of my first quilt show, following the order handed down by my guide, Sarah, I find myself—very much to my surprise—revisiting the concept of needle and thread, this time as something I might conquer. Or at least not be conquered by.

The Supreme Quilt Being happens to be smiling upon me this particular day. Nervously I approach the beginners' table, which is set up each year at IQF to acquaint the uninitiated with the most basic quilting lesson. No machines here. No Mrs. Haggard either. Instead Mary Geehan, a soft-spoken woman with a gentle Irish lilt, welcomes me. Now, a brogue is as appealing to me as sewing is not (or was not at that point). Pulled by the sound of her voice, I sit.

"You're going to make a four-patch," she informs me, holding up a sample block of four little squares sewn together. "This is what it's going to look like when it's finished."

Now she sets me up with four little squares—two white, two pale blue with flowers and butterflies—which clearly are not sewn together. Which means somebody has to do it.

"The first thing you want to do is turn it to the wrong side of the fabric," she says. I flip the blue squares, having been informed there was no "wrong" side for the plain white. Mary hands me a little ruler and a pencil. "You want to draw—this is a quarter-inch line—you're going to draw a quarter of an inch the whole way round on all four."

Immediately I am nervous, which means I begin to ask questions.

"Am I pressing down too hard?"

Mary doesn't answer this, because first she needs to point out that, even with the aid of a clearly demarcated ruler, I am not managing to draw my quarter-inch lines properly. Big surprise. "You want your line right to the edge," she says, as patient as a mother coaxing a child through a first potty training lesson.

"Perhaps I should get my glasses out," I say and laugh a little too loud. Then I mention, as casually as I can, that I thrive on praise. Finally, I resort to another question, hoping to divert Mary from paying too much attention to my lame quarter-inch attempts. "How long have you been quilting?" I ask.

"I've been quilting about six years. I've been sewing since I was about five years old," she tells me.

I love just about everything about quilting. The creativity, the tactile part of feeling the fabrics, the colors, the challenge of making things "fit," meeting the other quilters and socializing with them, and the sharing nature of quilters.

My husband's family were European immigrants. They found a common bond in quilting, even when language was a problem. Many years later, his Russian aunt, the last of the quilters from that group, decided to make a quilt for each of the women in the family, including in-laws.

She chose to make Double Wedding Ring quilts in the favorite scrappy colors of each woman. She even took her first plane ride at the age of seventy-seven to come to visit us in Pittsburgh, Pennsylvania, to determine what colors to make mine. This is considered a fairly difficult pattern, but she had a free template that she had drawn out of the newspaper, so she carefully traced it onto cardboard and laboriously cut each piece with scissors to make a total of 17 quilts— one for each of us.

After they were done, she hand-quilted each of them and arranged for a party for all of the "girls." No one knew what she had been working on for two to three years, so we were all completely surprised and thrilled to get our very own quilts from her. This labor of love inspired me to learn to quilt and to make quilts for my own family. —Ellen Cabluck, Austin, Texas

---

I've got my lines drawn. It's time to thread the needle. And now, oh God, she wants me to sew one little square to another. Now it's her turn to distract me from my phobia. She's telling me she lives in Houston but she lived in Alaska before that. Alaska is where she learned to quilt. "It was something I always wanted to do," she says. "It was something to do in the dark snowy cold. So I took one class. I love it. I find it relaxing."

"Is that far up enough?" I ask of my technique. "You keep telling me, and I keep forgetting."

She sets me back on course and never states what we both know—the ten stitches I need to complete Phase One here, she could've pushed through in three seconds. I'm still working until, eventually, I move on to my next two squares. For my next distracting move, I ask if there are a lot of quilters in Ireland.

"There is a quilting movement—I'm not sure how big it is. My sister never used to sew—she never picked up a needle in her life. Then my mother said, 'You have to see this quilt your sister made.' And she said, 'My God, my sister made a quilt? If she can do it, I can do it.' That's why I'm saying anyone can do it. My very first quilt that I made, I cut six-inch squares, all different colors of fabrics, and I sewed them all together and that was my first quilt. I did it by machine."

Now, when Mary tells me this, even though I'm sitting here looking at two-inch squares, even though I've just looked at well over a thousand quilts, many of them featuring blocks of tiny squares, it doesn't register what she's explaining to me. Six-inch squares are to quilting what Lane Bryant is to women's clothing. Six-inch squares should be a relatively easy project. But just getting these four pieces together seems like it might take me all day. I will never really be a quilter.

Undaunted by the negative vibe I'm emanating, Mary cheerfully points to my two pairs of two squares and announces, "Now you're going to put the right sides together."

I obey, putting the two faces together. Again I fumble attempting to rethread the needle. "Will you show me how you knot it?"

"There's all different ways," she says. How I love that accent. That accent is responsible for keeping me here, keeping me calm, like a Valium taken before boarding a plane. "I'll show you the way I knot it. You hold it between your finger and thumb and wrap it round twice and through the loop. And you can just clip off the end of it."

She offers me a thimble, but I decline, citing a joy-in-pain streak I have, hoping she can tell I'm attempting, yet again, to be funny. She shows me how to stitch the two pieces together so I'll have a nice little checkered pattern—blue patch, white patch up top; white patch, blue patch down bottom. I watch her push the needle in and out several times, gathering material on it, rather than a stitch in, a stitch out. This amazes me.

"As many as you can fit?" I ask. "I never thought about it like that."

"In time the stitches will get smaller as well," she says.

"You're saying I have big stitches?!" I ask. I'm teasing her. Sort of.

"No, no," she laughs. "I said you can get smaller . . ."

"I'm defensive," I defend.

"I know you are!" she laughs.

"My mom's going to be so delighted."

"You can send it to her. One of the kids that was here, I asked her what she was going to do with hers. She said, 'Ah, I think I'll make a diaper with it.'"

I reach the end of my seam, and confusion returns. "I keep going?"

"You stop and do a double stitch."

"Do I go to the very edge?"

"You don't necessarily."

"And now what?"

"You cut your thread."

"I don't have to tie an elaborate knot?"

"A double stitch should do."

I prepare to do the remaining three sides, and then I have a light bulb moment. "Oh! I don't have to sew all four sides!" I observe.

"If you do all four sides, you won't be able to do anything with it!" Now Mary really is laughing. It turns out I am quite possibly the thickest student she's had all day—I was going to sew my four square shut.

"You're getting paid a lot of money to do this, right?" I ask.

"Yeah, right." She laughs again.

"My God! Look at that craftsmanship!" I say, offering up for her approval my finished top piece, all four by four inches of it.

"Isn't it beautiful?" she asks.

"It's my new calling."

"That's a basic four-patch," she says, reaching over to a pile and retrieving a little square of batting and a little square of solid material for the backing. Miraculously, I have another light bulb moment—two inside of five minutes here, maybe this *is* my new calling—as I remember that Sarah had explained to me the three basic parts of a quilt.

"Ohhhh, it's ringing a bell now," I say.

She shows me how to mark the squares before putting them on the backing. I trace a little heart stencil on the top right white square and the bottom left white square.

"You can baste it now. Basting are just long tacking stitches," she explains.

"My specialty. Am I going to pin this?"

"You can pin it. It just makes it easier. This is the point when you want to make sure you really get it flat. At this size it's really easy. The best thing to do when you're doing a larger quilt is to put this backing layer on the table and use tape like masking tape—that keeps it in place. And you do it the same until you get all the layers down. That makes it much easier."

I try to follow instructions, but I think I miss. "I bunched it up, didn't I?"

Mary isn't too worried about these minor gaffes of mine. She keeps prompting me to forge ahead. Maybe she wants to get rid of me? But at least I'm the devil she knows. Who might come after me? A nonverbal two year-old? Someone with a permanent quiver in her hand? *A man?!!*

"Now you're ready to hand-quilt. This is more the sort of thread you'd use to pull through. This one you're just going to do one knot. You want to bury the thread in the fabric. You start by putting the needle in—the top and maybe the second layer. Bring it up on the line, and then you pull your knot totally through. This way can't see it. You put the needle in and use the thimble. You get maybe two or three stitches, and you just go all the way around your little heart."

Ah, yes, my little heart. I spare her a bad joke about bad boyfriends and carefully work my way around the heart, through the top and batting and back, then back up again. I get to the top. "On a curve it's a little more difficult?" I ask, hopeful, looking for an excuse for my shoddy workmanship.

"Not really. You just do smaller stitches." Ah, once again Mary is trying to subliminally plant the smaller-stitches message in my stubborn head. I do the best I can. It puckers. But I did it. I quilted.

Now, if I can just go home and transfer this newfound confidence to the sewing machine I borrowed from the wife of an old ex-boyfriend.

3

Seams Challenging Enough

Back from IQF 2002, eagerness and wariness each push valiantly for a foothold in the pincushion of my heart. I'm still bearing a post-fest afterglow. The fabric I purchased—superbold flannels, bright patterned in tie-dyed-looking oranges and greens, teals and blues—still makes me incredibly happy to admire and run between my fingers.

But there are a couple of problems. First, I haven't bought enough fabric to make a decent-sized top piece. Second, I can't exactly go back and pick up more of the same—the show is over, the vendor is gone. So I'll need to hit the local fabric stores and dig through Sarah's bag of scraps to see what I can find to, hopefully, match what I've got. And third, I've picked flannel for my first fabric.

I love flannel. I wear flannel pajama bottoms about 90 percent of the time and that includes when I am out of the house, shopping, meeting with friends, dropping my son off for school. If flannel were a man, I'd've been happily married decades ago. Flannel does it for me.

But, Sarah tells me gently, flannel does not do it for me if I am a first-time quilter with a phobia of sewing machines. It's not that there's a law against flannel for a quilt top. But unbeknownst to me at purchase time, flannel can be pretty tricky to work with in small patches.

My first quilt, made in about the same amount of time it would take a dedicated quilter to make forty much larger, much more detailed, much more carefully sewn quilts. And yet, it instills a deep sense of pride in its creator. Photo by Kakki Keenan.

Arlene Blackburn, standing in front of the original *Midnight in the Garden of Good and Elvis*, the quilt that was destroyed by bleach in an act of vengeance at the 2002 International Quilt Festival in Houston. Photo courtesy of Arlene Blackburn.

Bohemian Rhapsody, by Ricky Tims, the Caveman Quilter. This quilt won
first place for Innovative Appliqué (Large) at the 2002
International Quilt Festival in Houston. Photo courtesy of Ricky Tims.

Pink Flower Prelude, by Ricky Tims. Photo courtesy of Ricky Tims.

Precious Water, by Hollis Chatelain. This quilt took Best of Show at the 2004 International Quilt Festival in Houston. Inspired by a dream the artist had, it is painted with six values of yellow and quilted with more than two hundred colors of thread. Photo courtesy of Hollis Chatelain.

A Moment in the Shadows, by Deborah Sylvester. Photo courtesy of Deborah Sylvester.

Do You Dream in Color? by Deborah Sylvester. Photo courtesy of Deborah Sylvester.

Poised, by Inge Mardal and Steen Hougs. Winner of the Maywood Studio
Master Award for Innovative Artistry at the 2004 IQA Judged Show. Photo by Jim Lincoln.

River of Life, by Inge Mardal and Steen Hougs. Winner of the Fairfield Master
Award for Contemporary Artistry at the 2005 IQA Judged Show. Photo by Jim Lincoln.

Pit Stop, by Inge Mardal and Steen Hougs. First place for two-person quilt, 2004 IQA Judged Show. Photo by Jim Lincoln.

Ringed, by Inge Mardal and Steen Hougs. First place for two-person quilt, 2005 IQA Judged Show. Photo by Jim Lincoln.

Debra Armstrong's *Victorian Crazy Quilt*, photographed on the porch
of her Victorian home in Lockhart, Texas. Photo by Eli Durst.

Sarah has a solution. Why not start with a comforter? Her kids love all the fluffy flannel comforters she makes. My kid surely will love one if I make it. And comforters are sort of the tricycles of the quilt world—while the process does involve sewing squares together, the squares are much bigger and easier to handle than the little pieces that go into quilt blocks. It'll be good practice learning to sew those quarter-inch seams with a machine. And even before I begin sewing, it'll be good practice with the ruler and rotary cutter, learning how to cut straight lines while avoiding slicing a tendon or major vein.

Okay then, we're on. I bring my borrowed machine over to Sarah's house and set it up near hers. She shows me the parts. I hand her my nice, new, expensive thread, in colors to match the fabric. "It's very pretty," she says. "But so you know next time, thread doesn't show for the seams—you can use the gray stuff. You save the pretty thread for the actual quilting."

Oh.

But Sarah, who knows how sensitive I am in general and how especially sensitive I am given my eighth-grade wrap-around-skirt fiasco, measures her words carefully. She's not here to bring me down, man. She is here to make a quilter out of me. But first, the rotary cutter.

Having done fifteen years of food service, many of them in pizza restaurants, I am well familiar with the kitchen cousin of the rotary cutter: the pizza cutter. Sarah shows me how to measure off and cut five-and-a-half-inch squares of the fabric, using her clear plastic gridded quilt ruler and the cutter. She then sits and sews—she's working on a project in all blues, with parallelogram-centered blocks—while I stand at the Ping-Pong table (a.k.a. sewing table) and cut. And cut. And cut.

And swear.

Damn.

It seems like, given such accurate equipment, this should be easy. Somehow, though, not all of my squares are exactly the same size. Sometimes I stop and trim them. Other times I let them slide and toss them in the pile. I know this is an exact art. This is part of the reason I'm convinced I'll fail. Or at least produce some pretty unwieldy results.

I'll need time squeezed out over a number of afternoons and evenings to cut all of my squares. The extra fabric I bought at the fabric store to make the whole thing big enough is plain yellow and plain light purple flannel. It looks dull compared to my original choices. Not only that but there is so much more of this yellow, this purple. I try not to think about how that's going to look, how it's going to rob the comforter of my original all-bright, all-bold vision. But the fabric store didn't have anything even close to what I wanted. I settled. Not the first time in my life.

Finally, it's time to sew. Sarah goes over the parts again, shows me how to wind a bobbin and thread the machine. Here's the presser foot. Here's the foot pedal. Here's a pair of flannel squares. Now *sew.*

Sew? But. But. But.

Sew.

This is the moment I knew would happen but swore would not. I put the patch-atop-patch (right sides in) down on the area near the needle, flip the presser foot, hit the gas. *Whe-whe-whe-whe-whewhewhehwhewhe.* First seam finished.

"Look!" I hold up my first patch, triumphant.

"Good," says Sarah, glancing up from where she's whizzing through her project.

Like the cutting, the sewing will take some time. Eventually I move the machine back to my house, convinced I have mastered the quarter-inch seam. Then one day, with maybe two patches left to sew, the bobbin runs out of thread.

I try ten different variations trying to figure out how to rethread it. I stop short of using the dogs as a part of this experiment. I fail every time. I left the instruction book at Sarah's. I call her to ask if she has it. She put it in a pile. She can't find it. She can come over and help me, but not tonight. I want help right now. Impossible. I set the project aside.

Eventually Sarah shows up, a week or two later. She reminds me of bobbin technique, sets me back up, gets me going. It might be too late, though. Now I walk past the sewing machine like it's a homeless person I've given change to too many times. I'm desensitized. I can't whip myself into a frenzy anymore. A pile of patches, too many of them purple and yellow, withers in the basket beside the machine.

Until one night, the switch flips on. Something seizes me. I head for the sewing machine. It's going to be a very long night—a jet-lag evening, as I like to tell my son, when suddenly I am wide awake at the oddest hour, burst of energy prompting me to re-attend to that which has been neglected.

I'd like to say I finished the comforter that very night. Are you seeing a pattern about me, then—this ongoing desire to begin and finish a project in a single sitting, no matter how big that project is, no matter how detailed? I discover as my sewing experiment goes on that beginning quilting is much like parenting in that it involves what I call forced patience. Anyone who's ever dealt with a fussy infant, a cranky toddler, or a surly teenager knows you can grow as impatient as you'd like in response. And, too, you can watch as your impatience in dealing with the problem proves as effective as dousing a fire with turpen-

---

I started quilting in the seventies because I was poor and I needed blankets. I saved all the fabric and I had scraps, and that's why it was more economical to make a quilt than buy a blanket, because I didn't have to buy anything except the batting. So that's how I started, and then I stopped.

When I moved to Texas, I came to a quilt show in 1988, the Austin show, and I just couldn't believe how quilting had changed, and it just hit a spark. So I had the skills—I just didn't use them. And then I just started to push myself.

Each time I try to do something I haven't done before. So when I started making quilts in Texas, I started with all solid fabrics because I didn't know how I could mix prints. Then once I did that, then I started with Cathedral Windows. It's very easy, but it's time-consuming.

I'm really not very good at actual quilting. With the Cathedral Window, you don't need to quilt it; there's no batting. So the first quilt that I made with Cathedral Windows was just a Cathedral Window, and I didn't know how to do anything else. And then I started putting borders on them and then carrying these bits out into the border. Each time I've made a quilt, I've tried to do something that I haven't done before, to see if I can.

I have had some pretty good successes. You can't depend on winning an award ever. I've always kept my expectations low.

I have one hanging in the living room, a very small one that's called January '93, and it's sort of a catharsis quilt. January of 1993, it was the worst month in my family's history, and that's saying something—my nephew caught fire, my sister almost died, my mother lost her job. Some good things happened too. One of my nephews was chosen to play in the inaugural parade, and I got to know another nephew a lot better than I had, because I took him to the hotel with me while his mom was in the hospital.

So I made this small quilt that's sort of a catharsis quilt to get all of that negative feeling out, and it works. —Mary Shepherd, Austin Area Quilt Guild

tine. Sooner or later, like it or not, you have to calm down and face the situation realistically.

I can't tell you how long it took me to stop blaming the fabric, the thread, the machine, and sundry other inanimate objects for my ongoing failures—crooked seams, broken needles, uneven squares. But somehow I finally managed to sew first pairs of squares, then strips of squares, and, at last, the entire top. Which left me at a crossroads I would revisit more than once as I continued my journey, moving toward making not just a comforter but an Honest-to-Pete quilt. This intersection was clearly labeled. Time and again when I wasn't personally the biggest obstacle in my own path, I found myself standing at the corner of two extremely busy streets known as My Schedule and Sarah's Schedule.

The short version of my schedule looks like this. I'm a single mother to an active teenager whose father lives a thousand miles away. Which means I don't get breaks on Wednesdays or Sundays. I also work about twenty small jobs—teaching writing workshops and literature classes at numerous schools throughout the district. I also have a big job: freelance writer. And I've been blessed with roughly forty thousand friends (in town) and another two hundred and forty thousand with whom I communicate via phone and email.

On top of this, I have a medical condition called Overvolunteerism, which is caused by the Sucker Gene, which runs deep in my family tree. Having OV means those extremely rare moments that aren't consumed by running a house, raising a kid, working several jobs, maintaining treasured friendships, walking the dogs, and working on the Great American Novel, must—absolutely must—be filled with doing work for the PTA, starting up a project to teach kids to knit, leading junior high writing clubs, protesting the war, etc. Which means that, in a typical year, I have about seven and a half minutes for hobbies like reading, knitting, sleeping, and, now, quilting.

Which is nothing compared to Sarah, who has two kids (three if you count her husband, Phil), a high-powered attorney job with the State of Texas, an elderly mother with cancer, an older mentally retarded brother she cares for, and a much more dire case of OV, which often finds her not merely volunteering but spearheading other volunteers as she takes on positions like PTA president and chairwoman of the Halloween carnival.

So here is how the cycle came to look: I would fear, and thus avoid, sewing.

I would fight back my fear and sew a little. I would suddenly sew for thirty minutes to an hour and decide I wasn't afraid of sewing after all. I would set aside other duties—"Son, I need you to feed yourself and do your own damn laundry"—and immerse myself in sewing until I required Sarah's guidance for the next step. Then I would have to set aside my project and wait for her to have time. Which could, literally, take months.

I suppose I could've signed up for a class or gotten a book and taught myself. I have to say I often find classes off-putting for a number of reasons. One is that I grew up in a group and mostly try to avoid groups as a result. Another is that, even though I myself am a teacher, I have this concern that if I take a class, I'll be laughed at. Mostly this is unfounded, but remember I was talking about Mrs. Haggard and how she cringed at my sewing? I never wanted that to happen again. Sarah, a friend for years who understood my quirks, seemed worth waiting for.

So I would wait. And wait. At least with the comforter, we did get to it within eight months, stretching it across her Ping-Pong table and tying it. I admit Sarah did most of the work, partly because it was at her house and so she'd get to it while watching the news. And also because she was much faster. The part of me that likes to brag, like a first grader, that I completed a project on my own felt some minor resentment at being assisted. But the grown-up, time-challenged, knot-tying-challenged side of me was nothing but grateful. When at last the project was finished, I felt a true deep satisfaction when I woke my son, Henry, up in the mornings, finding him curled beneath all those brightly colored flannel squares, even the yellow and purple ones in their (previously) annoying abundance.

Bolstered by this sight, I decided to forge ahead. Sarah said she knew just the project I should work on next, digging around on the Internet to find good examples of the scrapaholic pattern, which she then sketched out for me on an index card. I tacked this on the wall above my sewing table, upon which now sat my very own sewing machine. I'd returned the one I borrowed from my ex-boyfriend's wife and replaced it with an ancient, five-hundred-pound Kenmore, purchased in mint condition from a thrift store for less than a hundred bucks. And then, once again, I set my mind to cutting out my squares and, perhaps more importantly, actually locating the time in my schedule to conquer this task.

4

My First *Real* Quilt (An Attempt)

I confess that there are times—many of them—when I approach things in a backwards fashion. I'm certain I'm not alone in this. For example, I meet people all the time who ask me, "How can I get an agent for my book?"

"Your book?" I'll ask.

"Well, I have an idea for a book."

I know what they mean by this. They mean that they dream of having a book published. The book they dream of having published is in their head. Or maybe just the idea for it is in their head. And they figure the first step is to get an agent who they figure will instantly love their idea and sell it to a book publisher for a big fat six-figure advance so they can live high on the hog while writing the book. The next part of the fantasy involves them taking a glamorous book tour, which includes five-star hotels around the world, selling millions of copies in dozens of languages, and fending off countless swooning fans clamoring for autographs.

But I'd say about 85 percent or more of the people who ask me how to get an agent for their book haven't written a single word of that book yet. And most don't actually write at all. They wish they wrote. Or at least they think they wish they wrote. There's a famous saying that goes like this: Everyone wants to say

My first quilt, made in about the same amount of time it would take a dedicated quilter to make forty much larger, much more detailed, much more carefully sewn quilts. And yet, it instills a deep sense of pride in its creator. Photo by Kakki Keenan.

they've written a book, but few people want to do the work it takes to actually write a book.

I'm not one of those people. I enjoy writing books. I'm familiar with the process and with the reality—that big advances are rare, that not all books that get written get published, and that producing a finished product can be painstaking and all-consuming. Fortunately for me, the process is also completely addictive.

You would think then, after more than twenty years at it, I would have learned enough humbling lessons about patience and taking baby steps and keeping expectations low when it comes to writing. And you might also think I'd gained even Great Wisdom and come to understand that such lessons can be helpful in all areas of life.

And if you thought these things about me, you'd be wrong. Particularly when it comes to quilting. Because when I decided I would learn how to quilt,

I was exactly like those nonwriters who approach me, certain they are the next William Shakespeare or Stephen King or Danielle Steele. Just as others want to magically produce a book without first learning some rudimentary writing skills, I pictured myself sitting down at the sewing machine, hitting the gas, and speeding my way to a stunning masterpiece. Hopefully in a week or less. All my friends would bow down in awe at my natural talent, which, for forty years, had lain dormant, just waiting to be discovered.

"*Wow*, can you believe that's her first quilt?!" friends and strangers alike would loudly whisper, standing in front of my Best of Show winner at the International Quilt Fest. Their excitement for me would mix with jealousy as they envied my skill and my overnight success.

Wait, back up. The truth is, I knew I wouldn't produce anything worthy of an award, not at first and probably not ever. I was well aware of my sewing phobia and recognized from the start that this would be a major obstacle. But I also envisioned conquering the phobia and mastering the machine. Just as we've all imagined what it would be like if we were famous or weighed less or won the lottery or had some extra something in our life that we felt certain would bring us instant happiness, I could imagine what it would be like if I could suddenly and effortlessly quilt.

Almost immediately upon deciding to become a quilter, I developed a case of Quilter's Eye, whereupon everything you look at, from up close or faraway, becomes an idea for a quilt. For example, swimming laps at the Y, I'd envision a bird's-eye view of the pool and in my mind translate this to a quilt with a built-in-pool blue background with strips of black fabric demarcating the lanes and colorful circles representing swim caps and equally colorful triangles repre-

---

I never took a class—just watched Alex Anderson for about six months, bought a couple of books, and asked my mom a few questions. I joined a block-of-the-month, read the directions, and began. My quarter-inch seam came out a little too large, so I got my ruler and rotary cutter out and "fixed" my seam so it would measure one-fourth inch. I was so proud of myself—I "fixed" several of my blocks this way and did not discover how incredibly stupid this was until I went to square up the blocks, and they are too small. Thankfully the quilt is scrappy and I'll be able to fix them, but that is the biggest mistake I have ever made (so far). —Sheryl Dickerson, Benbrook, Texas

---

senting those flags they put up to keep you from smashing your head into the wall during a backstroke.

Which is to say that, as others are ignited by the thought of writing a book, so I was ignited by the thought of creating a quilt, and I was eager—overeager even—to get the first one done. Let me say, in my defense, that the flip side of this impatience coin, which has ruled much of my life, is enthusiasm. It's not that I think I am perfect and thus should have been able to just sit down and sew perfectly. It's just that, when I see something I like, I wish I could do it, not later, but *immediately*. It's very difficult for me to accept the fact that most things we desire to learn require dealing with a learning curve.

As with most of life's great lessons, though, I found out the hard way. That original desire to get going and quilt, quilt, quilt visited me in late 2002, not long after my first International Quilt Festival. Almost as quickly a bad case of unintentional procrastination struck me down. I didn't cut my first fabric for another several months. Then, while I was engaged in the cutting, my focus was intense and I stuck with it for days. But when I set aside my work, I found that returning to the task was difficult. Life continuously got in the way.

Instead of squeezing in a few minutes each day to work on my quilt, I kept fantasizing that a large block of time would present itself to me. During this fantasy time block, the phone wouldn't ring, my son wouldn't need a ride anywhere, no email would arrive, total silence and peace would prevail, and a secret patron would anonymously send envelopes stuffed with cash so I wouldn't have to waste my time working at my job. I even imagined that my mind—forever racing with never-ending to-do lists—would quiet down. And there I would go, cutting, sewing, quilting.

Are you laughing yet?

As I sit here writing this, nearly two years have passed since I first imagined myself a quilter. That first quilt isn't finished yet, though it is getting there. Before I tell the tale of that quilt's slow gestation though, I must first tell of the masterpiece that came to be my true first quilt. What I mean is, I set aside my *first* first quilt—due to a variety of circumstances beyond mere procrastination—and proceeded to make my second quilt with much less difficulty. And, in fact, keeping in line with my original vision, this second-quilt-which-turned-out-to-be-my-first-quilt, I did manage to finish in a single day. (This reminds me of an old joke about a couple deciding to skip their first date and begin their romance with their second date, since second dates are more relaxing.)

How did I accomplish such a feat? Did a miracle take place whereby I woke up one morning a savant, able to quilt at will? Did I hire someone to do my work for me? No. The truth is, I took a few blocks I had left over from my first first quilt, sewed them together sloppily, slapped on some batting and a back, and sewed the way I wanted to: as fast as possible. I sat there, listening to Bob Marley, singing along loudly to his lyrics, which I'd altered to suit my needs. Instead of singing "Everything is gonna be all right," I sang "Every seam is gonna be all right."

I felt release and relief as I whizzed along. I giggled at a pun that popped into my head, "You reap what you sew." Kenta, a twenty-year-old Japanese exchange student living with me at the time, sat nearby watching, clearly amused. Every seam or so, I'd hold up my work. "Very good," he would praise, falsely but sweetly.

It wasn't very good. It was a mess. I didn't have an embroidery foot. I sewed "straight" seams (very crooked ones) along the seams of the blocks. If fabric bunched up, I told myself aggressive pressing would rectify it later. In short, I became a speed quilter, my end-product maybe one foot by two feet. I was totally delighted. I even came up with a motto for my new technique—*What I lack in skill, I make up for with speed!*

I confess I waited another week or so to do the border, which I created not with new strips of fabric but merely by folding over the excess of the back to the front, folding it in a second time, and sewing it with rather large, very visible stitches.

I focused. All else around me faded to the background. I hunched over my work, completely unaware that my thimble was on the wrong hand. (Sarah would point this out to me later, when I was working on another project in her presence. Her observation of my incorrect thimble usage went a long way toward answering my question, "Why do I even need this thing? I haven't stuck myself on this finger once!")

When it was truly finished, I presented this quilt to my soul mate, my late-in-life surprise puppy, Princess Bubbles, the Boston terrier mix. Bubbie immediately appreciated my handiwork, showing her satisfaction by falling back into the nap she briefly awoke from when I placed the quilt upon her royal little shoulders.

My house is very old and very small and is owned by a very old landlady who lives very far away. Part of our unspoken agreement is a sort of don't-ask, don't-tell policy. She doesn't ask me damning questions such as, "Say, you don't happen to have eleven pets on a one-pet lease, do you?" And I rarely ask her for home improvements or repairs despite the exorbitant rent I pay her.

This is one reason why my house is heated not with central heat but rather with a small gas furnace on the wall of the living room. (My bedroom is heated at times with a plug-in radiator but mostly with my pack piled around me in bed at night, making every night a three-dog night.) The gas furnace is sort of a cross between a tiny fireplace and an open campfire.

We don't get too many very cold nights in Austin, but when we do, Henry and the dogs and I often compete for the spot directly in front of the fire. Which is how Bubbles' little red quilt gravitated from her bed over to the spot on the floor that is, for all intents and purposes, the invisible hearth. It is there Bubbles naps upon the quilt, toasting herself into a cozy dream. It is also there where Bubbles awakes and goes through her stretching routine, which has caused me to nickname her quilt Bubbles' Yoga Mat.

Though that quilt has been part of my life for some time now, I still derive great joy and satisfaction every time I see it. Making it helped me break through the barrier and move from being a nonquilter to a quilter. Making it let me feel what it feels like to sew through three layers for a sustained period of time. (By "sustained," I mean the seventy seconds it took me to sew a seam lengthwise from one end to another.) Making it eliminated the need for me to have to deal

---

I give all my quilts away—it fills me with joy to present a quilt made with love with someone in mind.

There used to be a group of quilters who met in Bertram, Texas, since 1935 — they disbanded in 2000, alas. These women would get together monthly for three days to quilt.

Each month was another member's turn to put in a quilt. Once a year they sold the month to make a little money for their activities. I was lucky enough to have them quilt several quilts for me.

I worked full-time, so my interaction was limited, but one month I got to spend an entire day with them. They argued over every little thing! Late that afternoon, one of them said, "Beth is going to think we argue all the time."

I laughed—it was the only time they agreed on anything.

—Beth Lyda, Oatmeal, Texas

THE MYSTERIES OF QUILTING REVEALED

with weight control on my first project. And I hate weight control whether we're discussing my butt or the heaviness of a rolled-up basted quilt being maneuvered around the needle. Making it made me finally feel the joy of quilting that I had, by the time I actually made that thing, heard described countless times by other quilters.

And making it also got me over my Fear of Rotary Cutter hump. This, I think most quilters know, is a legitimate fear. Those rotary cutters are not to be taken lightly. I'd had just enough experience with mine—cutting out pieces for my first first quilt—to be dangerous. Fortunately I'd sat in, as an observer and reporter, on a quilting workshop where the teacher made a big deal about reminding us to ALWAYS be careful and NEVER pull or push a cutter toward the hand that was holding down the fabric. Had I not received that lecture, I probably would've cut myself sooner, and deeper, than I eventually did. .

I think I knew a cut was coming. Not to say I had a premonition that that very night it would happen. But more that I had a sense of inevitability. And when that blade hit my finger, I was flooded with numerous reactions. Indignation, shock, pain, and—to tell the truth—a measure of relief. I'd gotten through the first cut with all tendons and arteries intact. This was just a reminder from the universe to Pay Attention. I receive such reminders fairly regularly, and I try to take them for what they are: warnings of the blessing variety.

Cutting my finger didn't slow me down too much. I bandaged it and kept right on going, determined to finish my little quilt. As I went along, the blood pulsing palpably at the point of the laceration, I remembered an incident almost twenty years before when I worked in the deli of a grocery store during my senior year of college. There I sliced hundreds of pounds of boiled ham. I'm sure I sliced other meats, but in my memory the boiled ham is what sticks out. Pound upon pound upon pound. Sliced thin. No thinner than that. I'd watch that slicer blade and I'd think of stories of fingers lost and I'd just wait for my turn.

The anxiety proved greater than the reality, though. I finally did cut myself. But the machine was turned off. I was dismantling it for a cleaning. I nicked my finger. I can still feel the catch of my finger on the edge of that blade. A reminder: *Be careful. Pay attention. Take your time.*

I made another little quilt after that first little quilt. I gave this one to Bubbles too. It was a kit I picked up at a JoAnn fabric store. It was already marked down 50 percent, and I had a 40 percent coupon—one of those coupons JoAnn's seems to send me forty times a week—so the whole deal came out to about eight dollars. I remembered to be somewhat careful. I tried hard to pay attention. But once again, I failed to take my time. I whizzed through this one too.

It was my first appliqué project. I discovered the wonders of Wonder Under. I figured out how to zigzag on my machine. By the standards of others, my success was limited, but once again I was pleased with my results. Although the more I examined the pattern—a harnessed crow pulling a wagon of sunflowers—I kept getting this creepy feeling that somehow it was a metaphor for slavery. Creepy metaphors aside, I learned still more by doing. Better still, I was growing less afraid to experiment and take risks. Even though I was hardly a good quilter, it dawned on me that I was no longer terrified of sewing.

Sarah gets much of the credit for this. She's the one who started me on my first first quilt, choosing for me a scrapaholic pattern when I had no clue what I should begin with. As she promised, the blocks were easy enough to piece but left me with results that I could shape into something resembling a complicated geometric pattern. She showed me how to thread my old thrift store machine and fill the bobbin. She explained that I did not need to stop and cut the thread after each little piece was sewn to another little piece. These are all things that real quilters take so much for granted, like breathing, that I think they sometimes forget how daunting the sheer quantity of necessary starter knowledge is to newcomers.

Sarah didn't forget. She gave me the step-by-step lessons beautifully. Up until a point. And then Sarah's life and schedule got even crazier than it had been. Her first child was finishing high school and readying to go to an Ivy League school. Her boss quit, and Sarah had to temporarily take on a very heavy workload in a very stressful workplace. Her aging mother's health further deteriorated. I would find a rare free hour for a quilting lesson. She would be too busy. She would find a rare free hour. I would be too busy.

I got frustrated finally and went so far as to project some of my old sister baggage onto my good friend. Growing up, my three older sisters often banished me from the room during conversations they considered beyond my comprehension or worthiness. Being perpetually ostracized left me with a serious complex. The busier Sarah got, the more I blamed not finishing my first first quilt on her. When I did go to her house for a lesson one day, she set me to the task of safety-pin basting and went into another room to talk to her sister about their mother's illness. This pushed a button for me. In retrospect, it's easy to see I was being selfish. At the time, feelings from my childhood that, being a middle child, I would never *ever* be anyone's priority seized me.

I left Sarah's house hurt that day. The next day I retrieved my first first quilt from her place, melodramatically cursed myself for ever relying on anyone for anything and, more melodramatically still, purchased a hoop and hand quilting needles plus a couple of thimbles that I might or might not be able to figure out proper placement of. Fine, I told myself, *I'll just quilt the damn thing by hand.*

I pouted for a week. I fumed. Finally, Sarah called one night, and I burst out crying and told her how upset she'd made me. After many tears and the swapping of perspectives, Sarah got it through my head that this wasn't my childhood and she wasn't one of my older sisters banishing me from her presence. I apologized, and we agreed to move on. Soon after, she had me over to do some practice three-layer sewing, using scraps of fabric and batting and her fancy Bernina machine. She showed me how to stipple and told me to spell my name. I made a mess of it, but it was a fun mess. Best of all, I was actually quilting, if not on my first first quilt, at least on the scraps.

That was the lesson that sent me on my way, that gave me a whiff of what true quilting felt like. This reminded me of an expression an airline pilot friend once told me: "To learn how to fly into O'Hare in the rain, you have to fly into O'Hare in the rain." On one level this sounds like one of those goofy, faux-Confucius sayings you might find in a fortune cookie. But what he meant was, some things, you just have to do to know how to do them. Baptism by fire. You learn what you can from your trainers, but the rest of whatever you're learning—how that thing is supposed to really truly feel—well, you have to figure that out alone.

And so, armed with the little stippling lesson from Sarah, I returned to my old house and my old machine. And that is when I began, and quickly finished, my second first quilt, the Yoga Mat of Bubbles. That is when, in a manner of speaking, I first flew into O'Hare in the rain.

When my dad was getting really sick, I made him a fairly large lap quilt (he's tall) to keep over his legs. The afghan I made for him years ago was too heavy, but he was always cold. He really liked the quilt and kept it handy by his chair until the end. —Linda Hamlett, Georgetown, Texas

---

PART TWO

Meet the Quilters

*On the rough wet grass of the back yard my father and mother have
spread quilts. We all lie there, my mother, my father, my uncle,
my aunt, and I too am lying there. . . . They are not talking much,
and the talk is quiet, of nothing in particular, of nothing at all.
The stars are wide and alive, they seem each like a smile of great sweet-
ness, and they seem very near. All my people are larger bodies than mine
. . . with voices gentle and meaningless like the voices of sleeping birds.
One is an artist, he is living at home. One is a musician, she is living
at home. One is my mother who is good to me. One is my father who
is good to me. By some chance, here they are, all on this earth; and
who shall ever tell the sorrow of being on this earth, lying, on quilts,
on the grass, in a summer evening, among the sounds of the night.*

—JAMES AGEE, "KNOXVILLE: SUMMER 1915"

5

Felonius Punk

The happiness quota at IQF is very high. Crossing the threshold from the outside world—busy Houston streets—into the hullabaloo of quilts and quilters as far as the eye can see, attendees, even those returning for the fifteenth or twentieth time, experience the rush of a little child on Christmas morning. Visual stimulation is at a maximum, exciting fabrics and quilting accessories for purchase are in abundance, and portions up in the food court are XXL.

The responsibilities of home and family—demanding husbands, needy children, to-do lists, and bills—are all conveniently absent. And the spirit of Will Rogers hangs over the place—new friendships are formed in every ladies' room waiting line (and, with most men's rooms converted to ladies' rooms for the event, we're talking many, many lines), at every cash register, and with every inadvertent *oh-pardon-me-no-no-pardon-me-say-that's-a-lovely-quilted-vest-you're-wearing* brushing of the sleeves and bumping of bodies in the crowded, busy aisles.

With so much joy around every corner, it's pretty hard to imagine much sorrow at this festival. Even quilts commemorating lost loved ones, bat-

Arlene Blackburn, standing in front of the original *Midnight in the Garden of Good and Elvis*, the quilt that was destroyed by bleach in an act of vengeance at the 2002 International Quilt Festival in Houston. Photo courtesy of Arlene Blackburn.

tles with cancer, and the falling of the World Trade Center have more than a whiff of hope and honor about them. So when the news came that something truly awful had happened at IQF 2002, it seemed genuinely unbelievable, more so considering the details.

Rumors began spreading like peanut butter on hot toast on November 3, 2002, just after IQF wrapped up its most successful year to date. I got an e-mail from my friend Aaric, who happened to have a quilter friend who'd been at the show too and heard that a quilt had been intentionally, maliciously destroyed as an act of vengeance. Of his friend, Aaric wrote:

" She was even at the Houston show and told me an AMAZING story about some dude who sold a quilting machine—whatever the hell that is—to some woman. Not only did it not work properly, it burst into frigging flames. So she gets a replacement—and it zaps her with an electric shock. Being a proud American, she sues. He declares bankruptcy. At the show, he sees her, gets angry, and tosses a gallon of bleach on her award-winning quilt. Turns out that her quilt is worth enough to qualify him as a brand new felon. Yep, he's going to spend time in the pokey for Quilt Abuse.

The story was so preposterous I immediately dismissed it (with all due respect to the typically reliable Aaric) as urban myth. But the rumor persisted. Sarah called me the next day. Had I heard about the quilt show scandal? I logged on to quilts.com, and there was a notice about the unfortunate event from the IQF queen herself, Karey Bresenhan, director of the festival and cofounder of the International Quilt Association. In fact, Karey had two tragedies to report.

First, two quilts were stolen. One of these, *Rose Medallion*, took Gayle Anderson ten years to make. Whereas an analogy for such a loss might be the sudden death by heart attack of a loved one, what happened to Arlene Blackburn's quilt, *Midnight in the Garden of Good and Elvis* can only be seen as a brutal murder. As Bresenhan described the tragedy in her letter:

"The second incident occurred on Sunday, Nov. 3, at 5:00 p.m., just after Festival closed on the last day of the show but before the hall had been cleared of visitors. That's when a man wearing an exhibitor's badge threw bleach on Arlene Blackburn's quilt, *Midnight in the Garden of Good and Elvis*, in the IQA Judged Show. The bleach destroyed "Midnight." It was thrown with such force that it also splashed on the adjacent quilt, "Make an Appointment," by Amy Stewart Winsor, where, thankfully, it did less damage. (Ms. Winsor is hopeful that she will be able to repair her quilt.) This dreadful attack appears to be the premeditated act of a vengeful person who was carrying out a personal vendetta against Ms. Blackburn by ruining her quilt. As explained by Ms. Blackburn, this vendetta apparently stemmed from a pre-existing legal matter.

We have never before experienced such an incident with Judged Show quilts at Quilt Festival, and despite all our precautions, no one could have predicted this bizarre and hateful attack and none of our security precautions could have protected against it. After September 11, we tripled our security for the 2001 show and then decided to maintain security at that tripled level for this year's show, but even that extra effort could not prevent this deliberate act of destruction. We had two quilt guardians within twelve to fifteen feet of this man, and they could not move quickly enough to stop him. One of them actually saw the man throw the bleach and saw the bleach hit the quilt; this staff person, with no regard for his own safety, ran to the man, caught hold of him, saw his face, and reported his exhibitor's badge to be that of Dan Puckett of Design-a-Quilt (DAQ) from Paducah, Kentucky. The man broke free and ran away. Within 10 minutes, the officers from the Harris County Sheriff's Department who serve on our security force had apprehended Mr. Puckett. He was interrogated, arrested on a felony charge, taken to jail, and kept there for several days, at which time he was released on bail. Ms. Blackburn has been told that he will be prosecuted by the Harris County District Attorney's office to the fullest extent of the law.

I spoke to Arlene nearly two years after her quilt was destroyed, And though she does not want to be best known or most remembered for this event, she did agree to tell me her story which, over the years, took some even more bizarre turns. Here, in her own words, she recounts the tale to date:

" Seven years ago I didn't quilt a stitch, I didn't sew. I lived about two and a half hours south of Paducah. I'd just married, I had these two toddlers and new husband. I loaded them into a mini van and made them go to the AQS [American Quilter's Society] show. We walked through the entire show. I remember standing in front of this one quilt and going, *"I gotta learn how to do this."* I came home and got a machine and books and learned how to do it. Now I teach and I'm a full-time studio artist. I like the competitive aspect of quilting. It gives me a reason to get things done. I just strive to be the best that I can be technically. My background with architecture pulled me into this.

I had researched quilting machines—long-arm quilting machines and short-arm quilting machines—and I had decided I wanted a Gammill long-arm quilting machine. That's the top of the line. And I kept saying, "I want this. I want this, but it's fifteen thousand dollars." My husband, at Christmastime, gave me a Tiffany's box. Inside the lid he had written, "Get your Gammill."

I didn't want to do quilting for the public. I wanted it for my own personal use. So I was trying to find a way to get a cheaper machine. Design-a-Quilt had a machine that was moderately priced. It was only about five thousand dollars with all the bells and whistles. They were just south of Paducah, close to me. I thought, well, I can get service there, it's a cheaper machine, I wouldn't have to make some money off of it to have it—that type of thing. The next business day after Christmas, I called DAQ and ordered one of those rather than the Gammill. I ordered it over the phone. I had already test-driven it at a show and had done my research on it—I thought I had anyway.

I got it home. Three months after I bought it, it caught fire in my studio— started smoking and caught fire. It wasn't even my quilt. It was one of my best friend's, who'd driven over from Missouri. It started smoking within seconds. The thing is, you've pinned this whole quilt on there and it's rolled up, how to get the quilt off fast enough to save the quilt—forget the house. My husband had come home, and he basically yanked it off, not the quilt but the machine, because it's on a carriage.

So I called and asked for a refund on the machine because I had only owned it three months. I hadn't even done two quilts on it. And they wouldn't give me my money back. I was talking to Dan Puckett, the owner of the company. Well, he wouldn't give me my money back. I thought, "That's nuts." So I drove it to Paducah. They had just moved their showroom. It was the opening day of their new place and also the opening day of Quilt Show up there. And I had a quilt in the show that year too.

I went into the showroom. My mom gets kind of embarrassed with me when I go to return stuff. I was there two hours. He would wait on everybody

---

In 1976, I wanted to do something special for my in-laws' fiftieth wedding anniversary. I told all the relatives to embroider something on a square of white knit and I would put them all together. After finally gathering all the squares and piecing them together, I quilted them in really big stitches, even though I had never quilted anything before. If you are familiar with quilts today, you know we always use cotton fabrics and usually cotton batting. I used the fluffy nylon batting and used a sheet for the backing. However, the relatives and my in-laws thought it was wonderful so you don't always have to use good workmanship to get a message across.

Quilting is so much more than just putting pieces of cloth together. I have links to the future in all the quilts I make for and leave for my children. I started quilting because I loved old quilts and no one left any for me. I decided to make my own heirlooms. —Vada Boehme, Austin, Texas

---

but me. I said, "You're waiting on me." So finally he gave me a model off his showroom floor. All I wanted was a machine that worked—really, that was it. So finally I thought, "Okay, I'll go ahead and take a machine."

Not two months later, I go to turn it on—no warning—I put my hands on the handlebars, and it gave me an electrical shock so bad it knocked me back and left my right arm numb. I called him. And he wouldn't return my calls. I never spoke to that man again. Ever. He never called me. He never did anything. And so I wrote him a letter. Never any response. Finally I said, "It's five thousand dollars, and we live close enough to Paducah," so I called an attorney. I have friends up in Paducah. I called them and said, "Who's the best law firm in town? I'll get them to write a letter. Maybe if he gets a letter from an attorney, he'll give me my money back." So I did that.

Coinciding with that, I asked on the Internet—we have this quilt art group—and I just put the word out there. I just asked the question, and it was a neither-here-nor-there kind of a question—*Has anybody had any dealings with Design-a-Quilt? If you have, can you give me some information about the company?* I got three hundred responses in a six-hour period from seventy-six different users. They started flooding me with all this information. Turned out the fire thing happened to a lot of people. Then I started getting phone calls from people who had tracked me down. Most of these women were older. It turned into this thing where I had all of this information. In six hours I got this history of what had happened with this machine, all from a simple request.

I turned it all over to my attorneys. They wrote the letter, and he didn't respond. He was telling women on the phone—another woman who joined the suit with me, he had told her, "You're just a quilter. Nobody's going to listen to you. There's nothing you can do. You can't touch me." He was going to these shows and collecting money time and again, credit card numbers and everything and selling the stuff, and it was junk. And he knew all of the time he had all of these wiring problems. It was only a two-prong plug on the machine, so there wasn't even a grounding—it tells you how much I knew about it. It's just one of those things that you kick yourself [about] in hindsight.

So anyway, Dee Dobler calls me out of the blue. She's from South Carolina, and she's a hoot. She got her machine back—she had shipped her machine to him [for repair]. It came back looking like it'd been dropped from a two-story building right on the machine head, where the needle is. But the crate didn't have any metal shavings in it. It was totally boxed up—there wasn't any damage to the crate. He was trying to say, "It happened in shipping. Go ahead and file a claim for it." He had stitched on a piece of fabric—and stuck it underneath the needle—that said "I love you, Dee," and signed it "Dan" in stitching and put that in the box. It was creepy.

She called me, and I put her in touch with the attorneys. They ended up filing suit against him because he never responded to anything. He didn't show up in court. He's two blocks away from the courthouse, and he didn't show up. We won our suit against him. The judge found in our favor for faulty machinery.

Two days after we got our ruling and won our case against him—we won the value of the machine plus court costs and attorney fees ... he filed for bankruptcy and changed the name of his company and opened up and started going again, just transferred everything over. So we fought the bankruptcy on it. We said he's defrauding the federal bankruptcy courts.

He went to Houston and was selling machines in Houston [at IQF 2002]. It's hard sometimes to go to these shows—I just stay away from the area [where his booth is] because he is obviously a volatile person. He was at the show down there in Houston. It was my second year to have a quilt hanging at the show down there as a competitor. This was a quilt that I had made that hung at Graceland for the twenty-fifth anniversary of the death of Elvis. I'm not a crazy Elvis person—I say that with all due respect to the Elvis crazies, because they're great for our economy here—it was something I just made for that particular thing. So it had a monetary value because it had hung at Graceland.

I liked the way it turned out, so I entered it down there [Houston] and it was hanging there. I had a number of people who were interested in purchasing it from me, but I wasn't willing to let it go yet. It was really its first outing after Graceland. I'd finished it in August, so it was down there in October. I had a whole two years to ship it around and make money off of it from different shows. That's kind of the way it works ... you make one or two really good quilts that you want to compete with. Then you make your smaller pieces. You make your living off selling the smaller pieces. But you make your name for yourself with your bigger pieces that you're using for shows. It gets you teaching gigs and that kind of thing.

So it's hanging down there. I try to avoid his booth and everything, but on the opening night I didn't realize exactly where he was and there was this cool yarn booth I'd been dying to get to. I had to hit that before it got picked over. Well, I'm standing there, paying for about $350 in yarn—bad vice—and the woman who was ringing me up said, "Do you know the guy in the booth behind you?" and I said, "What?" She said, "Don't turn around, but he has been staring at you since you came into the booth."

I kind of looked over my shoulder, and Dan Puckett was standing right at the edge of his booth, just glaring at me and staring at me. Then he started yelling obscenities. I mean, I'm at a quilt show buying yarn . . . really ugly obscenities. I just kind of smiled a nervous smile and turned around and

There's probably a reason I'm a traditional quilter more so than some of our younger women, and that's because that's what it was when I grew up. Now, I've done innovative quilts and I've done a few art quilts, but it hasn't been my thing. So I decided I'm going to use what I really enjoy and do the best I can with that, rather than try to branch out.

I'm a third-generation Texas quiltmaker. My mother was a quilter, and my grandmother was a quilter. I married into a quiltmaking family. I had a wonderful association with my mother-in-law and quilts.

I learned to quilt as a teenager because my mother quilted on quilts we hung from the ceiling. I'm from a rural generation of farmers, and we make quilts for cover. I'm a Texan, but my parents moved me to Oklahoma when I was three years old and didn't ask me. Anyway, I learned to quilt when I was a teenager, but I didn't want to piece-quilt, so I learned to sew. My mother taught me to sew when I was about nine years old.

After I had my family, I sewed for my kids. When you come from a Depression-era generation, you save everything; you don't throw anything away. So when I created my own scrap bag, I finally decided, "Well, shoot, I'm going to do this." But because I had come from scrap quilts, one of the first quilts that I tried to piece I wanted to buy that material. And I did. I made a Lone Star quilt that I made with solid fabrics that I purchased. But after that I used scraps.

In 1961 my husband, who was in the National Guard, was called to active duty during the Berlin Crisis, and we chose to follow him to Fort Reilly,

— 38 —

finished paying for my stuff and just ignored him and avoided him for the rest of the show.

I was real excited my quilt had hung down there. It was great—I got a couple of teaching gigs from it. People like me to bring the quilt with me that hung at the show so other members of their guild can see it. It worked out really well, very positive—my mom had been with me the entire time and all my friends. On Sunday I got on the plane and came home in the afternoon, but before I did I actually went and walked down the aisle and looked at it one more time when the show opened on Sunday morning, just to see it hanging under the lights, and took some pictures. Then I went to the airport and got on the plane and came home, nothing the wiser.

Kansas. We couldn't find housing because the post was full. So we lived out in the country in a little farmhouse. My kids took a bus to school, and I had a three-year-old. So we stayed home on those winter days and just . . . it was the most desolate, lonely winter I ever spent. Well, I had moved all my scraps with me, so that winter I pieced quilts.

I quilted during the fifties and sixties, when it was not in fashion to do so. It's something I enjoyed doing and wanted to do. When this quilt revival started in the mid-seventies, we founded this guild here. I'm a charter member of this guild.

I never thought this revival would last. It's now about thirty-five years. It's the longest and the biggest quilting interest that's ever been. I just marvel at it.

For years every department store had a fabric department. They began to manufacture clothing, so people weren't buying fabric to make clothes. And so they began to shut down the fabric departments. When the polyester age came in the late sixties, you couldn't buy cottons very well at all. So when this quilt revival started, we had a hard time getting cotton fabrics. Little by little they began to manufacture more cotton. Now the home decorating industry and the quilting industry are the two main sources of the fabric industry. So the fabric companies gear their merchandise to quilters.

I've quilted a lot more than I've made, because I've had tops given to me. If I told you a number, you would think that's really a lot, but you'd have to understand, all the quilts I've made are not big quilts. They're little quilts—somewhere around three hundred. —Kathleen McCrady, Austin Area Quilt Guild

---

I hadn't been in the door five, ten minutes—I was just saying hey to my kids and my husband—I hadn't seen them for the week. And the phone rang, and my husband answers and says, "Arlene, it's Karey Bresenhan." She's, you know, head of the whole quilt show. I had just seen her a couple of days earlier. I thought, "Why on earth would Karey be calling me?" You know what goes through your mind is, "I did win! They *did* make a mistake!" That was so silly.

She goes, "Arlene I have some . . . some news for you." She said some officer was also on the phone. She said somebody had thrown bleach on my quilt, a vandal had thrown bleach on my quilt, right before they took it down.

"Oh, my God," I said. "Karey, I know who did it! I know who did it! It was Dan Puckett." I said, "Find him. Please have them find him." She goes, "Arlene, it's interesting that you would say that. The police have him in custody." I said, "Oh, thank God."

Then I asked if anybody was hurt or anything like that, and she said no, but that her staff had done everything they could to prevent him from doing it. They had roped off everything. Because he had his vendor's badge on, he was just kind of cutting through, the way vendors do when they go to get to their cars. He just waited for that moment. There were people and guards about every twelve feet on the show floor because when they take the show down, each one of these quilts is valued at such a high amount. You're talking about over a million dollars' worth of quilts. Mine was valued at $6,500, and it wasn't even a prizewinner. The guy saw him, with the drink container, get over the roped area to where my quilt was. This guy went running—he got him by the arm, but it was too late. He'd already made the forward motion to throw the bleach.

They wrestled him down and they saw— The guy is such an idiot. It said Dan Puckett Design-A-Quilt on his badge. He didn't even think enough to turn it around or take it off. He had his name tag on. So they wrestled him down, but he got up, broke free, and went running through the entire convention center. It was a driving rainstorm, and they found him out there— I think, underneath the trailer or something—and got him out and led him through the convention center in handcuffs. They had him in a holding room when they were calling me.

He was convicted of felony destruction of property, felony destruction of a

As part of her settlement against Dan Puckett, Arlene Blackburn received
the title to Puckett's classic Harley-Davidson. Here, she appears
on the bike with her attorney. Photo courtesy of Arlene Blackburn.

quilt. It was a Texas state felony the way it was charged. He actually went to
one of the worst prisons in Texas. You know, the only solace I really got in all
of this is knowing he went to a prison for something as stupid as what he was
arrested for. You know, "Whatcha in for, Bud?" "Destruction of a quilt."

To say I wasn't afraid of him, I would be fooling myself. I think he's a time
bomb. He's not responsible for his own actions. When asked why he did that
to my quilt, he said I made him do it, even though I didn't see him for the rest
of the show. He tells people I made him do it. He's not responsible for his
actions.

I wasn't going to let it consume me. But I didn't want to be the poster child
for idiocy. And I couldn't police the ignorance of others. You know I wasn't
going to tell everybody else, "These machines suck. They're going to catch
fire." I couldn't do that for everybody else. All I could do was take care of
myself in this matter. He took it public when he did that to my quilt.

The maximum payout that the festival would pay is $500 on the loss or
damage of a quilt. That was like another death. A quilt that took me eighteen
months. They sent me an empty box. But it had my judges' sheets, everything
I would've gotten, except the quilt was not in there. We got past that one too.

I have the quilt now, though. The weird thing is, when I got it back and I opened it up, everywhere the image of Elvis appears the bleach passed through and it's as bright and vivid as ever. There's an image of Elvis, this silhouette over the gates of Graceland kind of floating in the sky. That took the brunt of the bleach, but the bleach passed through all of it because it's bleached on the back. But the image of Elvis is just as bright as ever. It's bizarre to see.

I did remake the quilt in eight weeks. It debuted at the AQS show in Paducah. It gave me power. The postmark was the second of January. The quilt had to be totally done, the binding sewn, everything. I was crying on Christmas Eve. I thought I couldn't get it done. My husband came out to my studio and said, "You know, sometimes you just gotta let it go." I wasn't going to let him beat me. Because it was going to be my show quilt.

I got to the point where I wore my name tag backwards at shows. People would see my name, and they knew they knew it from somewhere. And you could just watch their face, and they put it together and they realized, "That was the quilt."

You know, I do so much more than that Elvis quilt. It was that one thing my husband had said to me as soon as I hung up the phone, "Well, I guess he instantly made a name for you. Everything you were struggling for." I had had business plans for two years down the road so people would know my name. He said, "Well, you got that one."

I made a book of all the e-mails that I received until I went through six copier ribbon things. People just started writing me, and some posted to websites. I really don't have the count, but it was probably well over two thousand messages that I got from people. It was like condolences for something that died. They were all very well-intentioned. I still run into people who will see my name, and they want to hug you. Quilters are a huggy bunch. And I'm not always that way. It's really embarrassing, kind of.

I have to say it made people aware of my work. They went to my website. This went beyond the quilting community. It went out into the art world. You have this unwanted association, but it also made people aware of what I do. I've made so many more contacts and friends than I would have if the incident hadn't happened.

My husband didn't say, "I told you so." He's so good. I have a Gammill Classic Plus now.

6

Caveman Quilting

"I can't do that. I just can't do it. No, I *can't*!" comes a cry of despair.

"I'll give you a certificate if you do," coaxes Ricky Tims, adding the gentle admonishment, "You're going to be so far behind if you don't."

More despair. "It hurts me to tear the fabric."

But tear the fabric she must if this reluctant quilter wants to succeed at the task she eagerly signed up to learn. She's one of a dozen quilters gathered in the Nassau Bay City Hall, across the street from Houston's Johnson Space Center, just down the road from the McDonald's with the huge astronaut on top. They've taken over council chambers, transformed the room into a temporary sewing paradise, and hired Tims, a.k.a. the Caveman Quilter, to teach them the art of Primitive Patchwork, a template-free, rule-breaking style of an art form that typically relies heavily on precise measuring.

Up at the long, somber desk usually reserved for council members, microphones have been moved to the floor, replaced with sewing machines and piles of cloth. Rows of chairs normally set out for the public have been stacked and pushed aside, making way for long folding tables upon which sit still more sewing machines and fabric stashes. These tools of

Bohemian Rhapsody, by Ricky Tims, the Caveman Quilter. This quilt won
first place for Innovative Appliqué (Large) at the 2002
International Quilt Festival in Houston. Photo courtesy of Ricky Tims.

Pink Flower Prelude, by Ricky Tims. Photo courtesy of Ricky Tims.

quilting await the nimble hands and creative forces of their owners, who, under Tims' guidance, are about to do some serious unlearning of techniques they've spent years honing. Before they begin, Tims explains his goal for this seven-hour workshop.

"I'm a quilter that's not in a box," he says. "I can make heirloom-quality, point-perfect quilts. But there are times when you don't need the pressure of making things exact, you just want to use your fabric because it's something you love, and you just want to play. I'm not trying to change the way you quilt. I just want to give you another way to quilt."

This information helps persuade, as does Tims' laughter-evoking point that, this being a Sunday, they can all be "holy tearers." Before long the room fills with the sound of rip, rip, ripping, the cacophony of several simultaneous conversations, and the distinct smell of irons heating up.

Decked out in Wranglers, plaid shirt, and Doc Martens, Tims stands at the center of this happy storm, alternately observing and chatting with his charges. He'll discuss where he was born and raised (Wichita Falls, Texas). He'll discuss his life in adopted home state (Colorado). And he'll break into song spontaneously—since the age of three, he's played the piano. Now he combines music, once his full-time career, with quilting anecdotes and history lessons into a program he presents to his students, who gush about his shows and collect his CDs. But he won't answer technical questions until day's end—this class is, among other things, a journey of self-discovery.

You can't help but notice that, gender-wise, Tims most certainly is outnumbered in his field. A survey commissioned in 2000 by *Quilter's Newsletter Magazine* reported that 99 percent of Dedicated Quilters, or DQs, are women. And while student Scott Philo skews that ratio in this particular class, the presence of eleven women nevertheless bears out the fact that almost only women quilt.

Of his minority status Tims says, "I want to play down that I'm a guy in a woman-dominated field. It's no different than a female working in a construction job—she needs to do a really good job to get the respect of her coworkers."

But Tims is neither naive nor delusional. "I realize there's a novelty aspect," he says. "I'm not going to deny the fact that maybe my career was spurred on by the fact that I'm a guy or happened a little quicker because

I'm a guy, and I hate that because I don't think it's the guy aspect of me that has made me have the success in the quilt world. I think it is the quilts I have made that have built my career."

That would be a hard point to argue. A year after he started quilting, Tims won his first award, a harbinger for a prize-studded career he stumbled into. Most recently, he won first place for Innovative Appliqué (Large) and second place for Merit Quilting at the 2002 International Quilt Festival in Houston. At the same festival, his *Songe d'Automne* took the Master Award for Machine Artistry.

"We were delighted to have the chance to acquire Ricky's 'breakthrough' quilt, *Songe d'Automne*, for our corporate collection," says Karey Bresenhan, adding, "Every major quilt artist has a 'breakthrough' quilt that puts her or him into the big leagues of art quilters, and that was Ricky's. It has beautiful hand-dyed cottons."

Tims is possibly as well known for his hand-dyed fabrics as his quilting. During the Primitive Patchwork workshop, participant Sharon Meyer offers curious noses a whiff of pieces she's purchased from his scented Delicious Fabrics line. A hot pink and electric yellow piece, Banana Strawberry, really does smell good enough to eat. (She says it gets even more fragrant when pressed.) The newest "flavor" is Blue Corn Tortilla, a dark, dusky blue.

Faye Anderson, another award-winning quilter from Colorado says, "I think whenever you come up with a new way of interpreting some aspect of quilting, it gets a lot of attention. What you do with the fabrics, especially when they're tie-dyed, can be challenging because the fabric can become the most important, which isn't always so good. He found a way to get his appliqué to blend in some places and stand out in others. I don't think we've seen this particular way of using the dyed fabrics before."

Anderson was an early influence on Tims, and he credits her for much of his success. At the first quilt meeting he ever attended, in Webster Groves, Missouri, she happened to be the guest speaker, discussing artistic design and quilting. (At that time, Tims was a choral director at a church in St. Louis.)

"Here's a lady speaking intelligently and scholarly on artistic design, and I'm sitting there going, 'Wait a minute. That's exactly the same thing I do to compose music.' Everything she brought out—rhythm, repetition—is the same thing that's in music. It was that night the seeds for formulating my own lecture were born."

That was in 1991. Just three months prior, Tims' then eighty-three-year-old grandmother had accepted a faraway marriage proposal, moved, and left him her old Kenmore sewing machine.

"On that first quilt I didn't know another quilter," he recalls. "All I had was a book. And the book said make templates, and I made cardboard templates out of cereal boxes and I drew around those templates on fabric with ballpoint pen. And it said cut out pieces with quarter-inch seam allowances, and I honestly thought it meant 'sort of.' I didn't know it meant 'Be accurate.' So my first quilt is rather pathetic, but it's still a treasure to me."

Not long after, he discovered rotary cutters. He used one to cut freehand curves, thinking, "I can just lay two fabrics down and cut them at the same time, and the two curves will fit into each other." He did not know enough about sewing to realize "real" quilters would've used a quarter-inch seam allowance. "So I had cut my little landscapey rolling hills, sewed the two pieces of fabric together, and when I opened them up, they weren't exactly flat. But I thought, 'Big deal. I'll just use a steam iron and press them flat.'"

Showing this quilt to that first guild, he found himself subjected to a grand inquisition by a suspicious quilter who, upon inspecting his unconventional style, told him, "You can't do that." Tims gave up on freeform then.

"Because I had met this quilt guild, I learned that there are rules, there are quilt police, there's a right way to do things and a wrong way to do things. So whatever I was doing in my freeness as an ignoramus, I ended up leaving that behind so I could learn to do it right. I went into the box, I learned to do it right, and for years that's the way I sewed. Everything was measured. If it was supposed to be two inches, it was exactly two inches."

It was during this time he met Suzanne Marshall, another self-taught award winner. Tims saw a quilt of hers hanging in a show at a St. Louis library. "He called me and said, 'I love your quilt, and I want to come over and learn how to make a quilt.' So he came over, and we've been friends ever since," says Marshall. "It's been so much fun to watch him develop and grow and become a force in the quilting world. And he is so giving himself in helping others find their creativity."

Once he mastered traditional quilting—the technique for which he wins awards—he revisited his original style and began teaching classes in which he encouraged students to cut without the aid of rulers. The resultant Primitive Patchwork (torn straight pieces) and Caveman Quilting (curves and "unorthodox pressing") classes took off.

Toward the end of this workshop, everyone has made noticeable progress, laying out their finished patches on different fabrics to decide on a background color. Margaret McPhail, a self-admitted type A engineer who has been gently ribbed all day as her co-quilters wonder if she can set her ruler aside, is trying out a deep chocolate. This is not her first class with Tims—she's taken the curvy Caveman class too. "It drove me nuts," she says. "Because he said, 'Just cut it. Put your straight edge away. The points do not have to be exactly right; the lines don't have to be exactly straight.' Actually, when you put it all together, the uniqueness of the curves and the variation and how they all go together make each one special. His quilts are very personable."

With just forty-five minutes left, Tims announces, "We have reached that point where you don't want to stop sewing." This is another way of saying it's time to stop sewing. As there was reluctance in the beginning, so there is at the end. But they stop to listen to his recommendations on which patterns to use when it's time to quilt the layers, and to hear his pointers on fabric dyeing. Once or twice during these closing comments, there is a sound, the quick zip of a machine as a formerly reluctant student, now hooked on Tims' Primitive style, sneaks in one last seam.

After attending Ricky's workshop that day—as an observer—not a quilter—I sat down with him for a talk. I'd watched him expend megawatts of energy all day and would not have been surprised to find my interview subject weary and not especially interested in being quizzed. Instead, he sat down with the same enthusiasm he'd exhibited for the preceding seven hours and talked at length about his life, his music, his art, his dreams, the quilting retreat he's building in Colorado, and the fact that he is a rooster in the henhouse, so to speak.

I never forgot that workshop, and the times I felt especially frustrated learning to quilt, I reminded myself of Ricky's first forays into fabric and his advice about not taking things too seriously and always remembering the blessing that is aggressive pressing. That advice continues to serve me well. Here are some thoughts Ricky shared with me:

"I started playing piano when I was three. I made an album when I was five of simple Christmas music, mostly for the family's benefit. It was my first language. I knew music and was reading music before I knew the alphabet.

I studied music at Midwestern State University in Wichita Falls, Texas. We had a tornado in 1979 that was really responsible for stopping my education. I ended up with seven years of college and 250 some odd credits but I didn't finish my degree. I was a piano major. Then I went to a composition major. And then, right as I was about to do my composition recital, we had the tornado and all of my compositions were gone with the wind. As a result of that, I went back to piano. But the teacher that I had studied with had retired and the new teacher that came in I just never felt connected, and my musical career was moving on. So even though I only lacked one elective and one recital, I stopped school and started out on my own, doing music. So all this education—I don't have the diploma in my hand.

In St. Louis, I conducted music at Kirk of the Hills Presbyterian Church. I was the music coordinator. My quilt guild is the Thimble and Thread Quilt Guild of Greater St. Louis. They meet at the Webster Groves Presbyterian Church. They claim me. Those dear sweet women in that guild. I resigned that conducting position in 1998 to specifically start doing quilting full-time.

Caveman quilting and Primitive quilting are similar because both of them are sort of nonmeasured. We're just cutting. We're just enjoying quilting—we're not worrying about measuring seam allowances and so forth. The main difference is in my Caveman class we're cutting and sewing those fabrics in order to create a small medallion style wall quilt. My goal is to teach them to cut and sew curves, gentle curves, without templates, without sewing with a quarter-inch seam, and there's some pretty unorthodox pressing methods, meaning press it until it's flat regardless of what you gotta do to make it flat. And that is not standard quilting. Typically you wouldn't want to distort your fabric.

Today's class, we didn't really deal with curves at all. Even though they cut freely without a ruler, they cut straight lines and they were creating geometric quilts that are more utilitarian, more functional, more quiltlike than artlike. So there's a difference in those two.

I discovered the rotary cutter by reading quilt magazines. And I started seeing them in a little fabric store—not a quilt store. So I thought maybe I should try this, because the second book I bought talked about strip piecing and using the rotary cutter and mat. I was amazed, because I had never seen a rotary cutter, at how beautifully it cut straight lines—you can't do that with scissors. You can't begin to do that with scissors. It's an eye-opener.

But I also—because I didn't come out of a home-ec background or a sewing background—I didn't have any rules to know, so I couldn't break any rules. What if I wanted to create a rolling hill, a little undulation? I can just lay two fabrics down and cut them at the same time, and the two curves will fit into each other. That's what should happen, but with the sewing you have to have a seam allowance. So just because you have two pieces of fabric that fit together when they're butted up doesn't mean they're going fit together when they're sewn, because of their seam allowances. I didn't know that either.

I remember taking that quilt to show-and-tell. I found a guild. The next meeting I brought this little quilt to them, and I showed it to them. And one of the ladies came up to me, and she said, "Well, how did you do this?" And I said, "Well, I just cut curves with the rotary cutter." She said, "But did you draw it out first?" And I said, "No, I just cut the curves and sewed it together." And she said, "Well, did you make templates?" I said, "No. I just cut the curves and sewed them together." She said, "When you cut the curves, did you include a seam allowance?" And I said, "No, I just cut them and sewed them together." And she said to me—I'll never forget—she said, "You can't do that." And I went, "Here's the quilt."

Well, I understand what she means—it's like a track. The inside track of a

---

I majored in math and minored in art, so I have this right brain/left brain thing going. Quilting is a nice outlet for my love of geometry, combined with playing with color, touching fabric, and sewing. I've always been into making things. Having an excuse to buy more fabric is good too. In the early days, I used to sit at work and design quilts a lot. Quilting is a relatively harmless outlet for us obsessive-compulsive types.

I got sick about eight years ago, and a lot of things in my life have changed. I haven't been quilting as much as before, but I'm also more relaxed about it. I think my best advice would be to enjoy it and not worry about the quilt police. I think I enjoy just getting something done now as much as I used to enjoy making something more spectacular in the old days.

—Beverly Howard, Austin, Texas

racetrack is small or a shorter distance than the outside. Because the curves are convex, there should be a seam allowance for them to fit. But fabric is forgiving especially if you're pressing. Even though it's not cut to fit exactly, it's at least similar enough that with a little bit of pressing it will work.

I wanted to learn to do it right. There were two reasons why I wanted to do it right. Number one, I wanted to challenge myself to excel. Why do things half-way? Number two, I think, comes into the dynamic I really often want to play down—that I'm a guy in a woman-dominated field. Because of that, I thought there was a need in me to excel, because my work was going to be scrutinized more. So I needed to do a better job so that if they looked at it, I had a little more respect. Now, that's a blanket statement; that's not everybody.

It was probably another three or four years before I started playing with this technique again. And then I ended up developing it into a class because I was starting to teach. At that time I had made these little quilts. I called them chantelles—these little tulips. I called them chantelles only because [when] I was teaching in England, I was observing a beginning quilting class. The next morning, the teacher of that class called with a funny story. She said, "You've gotta hear this. So-and-so wanted to know who Chantelle was."

I said, "What do you mean?" She said, "Ann brought Chantelle, and she was really confused because she thought she met everybody and she didn't meet Chantelle." And we all started chuckling—because, no, she didn't bring Chantelle; she brought show-and-tell. She misunderstood. So I ended up making this little tulip as a gift for my British hostess, and I called it *Tulip for Chantelle*, totally as a joke.

At the time I'm living in Missouri, which is the Show-Me State. So when I created the class, I called it "Show Me Chantelle," which is a silly name if you don't have any clue about Chantelle and if you don't know the slogan for Missouri. So for about nine months I taught "Show Me Chantelle" until one day, about two o'clock in the afternoon, a quilter in the back of the class shrieked and said, "This has got to be the way cavemen used to quilt. There's no measuring. There's no quarter-of-an-inch seam. This is just 'anything goes,' because they're not using any of those senses of intelligence." And so that's when I started naming it "Quilting Caveman Style." So anytime I'm doing something without a recipe, without really planning, without really measuring, just any old way—like when I'm dyeing fabric, if I'm just pouring the dyes on and there's no real recipe—I call it Caveman style.

I started quilting because I just wanted to make a quilt. I didn't have any idea that this was going to become a career or that I was going to excel or that it was going to change my life. That was never intended. I was a musician. My life was a musician—I'm going to be a musician forever. Quilting snuck in the back door and I was thirty-five years old or something like that, and now it's like changed my life.

Even though I say "quilting," I probably . . . If I look back on it, I never approached it because I wanted to make blankets for a bed. I have approached it from an aesthetic vantage point, and by approaching it from aesthetics, that to me creates art, visual art, visual aesthetics. The pieces that I make—it is a rare, rare, rare thing that I make a functional utility quilt for a bed. They're not designed that way. They're not meant to be seen that way. Mine are meant to be vertical, hanging pieces. Even if they're full size and look like they could fit on a bed, they're meant as aesthetic art. So therefore it doesn't feel so strange, because how would it be if someone said, "How does it feel to be a man artist?"

The only thing I can say is that I realize, I honestly realize that there's a novelty aspect to it. I understand that. So that if I make this and they say, "That's a guy—a guy made that," maybe people will perk up a little quicker. Maybe there will be a little bit more notoriety surrounding the fact that a guy did this, because it's at a quilt show and it's predominantly women.

The quilting world is so diverse now. It is so filled with "anything goes." If you're a quilt purist and you're a quilter that does hand quilts and believes that everything should be done by hand and it should be traditional patterns and you don't want to look at anything else, you're close-minded to that. I can't help that. But in general the quilt world accepts handwork, machine work, contemporary artwork, raw-edge stuff, people who will splatter ink on the quilt because it makes for a nice design. Anything goes. Raw-edge edge appliqué, turned-edge appliqué, fine quilting, rough quilting—it all has a place in the quilt world. So if it doesn't suit their fancy, they can turn their nose up at it, but it's not really a detriment.

I'm not doing anything really outlandish. Matter of fact, I pride myself in being an aesthetic art quilter trying to create these visual pieces. But I want . . . whenever Aunt Agnes, who has never done any contemporary quilting at all, walks up to the quilt and looks at the workmanship in it, she understands it, she can relate to it because it's using traditional—it's really pieced, it's really quilted, it's not glued here and tied on there and rough strings hanging off. Not that there's anything wrong with that. It's just that I try to stay appreciated by . . . there's a huge traditional streak. And part of that for me is, who pays my bills? I'm a working quilt artist. It's the quilt world, not the art world, that pays my bills. So why do I want to create something that doesn't relate to these people that I'm a part of? I'm not just doing that as a cognitive "Oh, I can't change." I'm doing what I love to do.

We all come from different backgrounds. And I realize in a class like today, whether it's Caveman or Primitive, there's unorthodox things going on and there are people that've worked hard to get to the level of expertise and workmanship—hard to get there—and then today I'm saying, "Oh, but don't worry about that. Rip the fabric." And so they're like, "I can't do this because it's going to demean what I've learned."

I don't want it to demean them. I just want to say "Hey, here's another way. And this is a fun way. This is playtime time—this isn't finesse time." There's a place for that, and I just want to encourage them and let them know there's a place and they don't need to feel bad if they're doing things that are technically less than they have advanced to in their own quilting skills. This is a simple class.

I work diligently when I'm home. I have two people at home that help me with the chores of life in the office work, doing the dye work, following up Web sales. A lot of the nitty-gritty of the work I do is taken care of by other people, so that leaves me the opportunity and the time when I'm home to be in a creative mode. And whether that's creating a quilt, creating and producing a video, writing or producing a book, only I can do those things, so I have to delegate responsibilities. It's been an incredible journey.

I made a very large quilt from neckties from all of the men in our family after my father passed away in 2000. When I was nearing the completion of my grief quilt, I had two of my sisters over to provide advice on the final assembly. As they stood over the pieces on the floor, they marveled and cooed while voicing the memory that each tie held—"Look, there is the tie that my husband wore at our wedding"; "Do you see that one? There's Dad's choir tie." And the memories that flooded back as my mom lovingly caressed her husband's ties . . .

—Mary Lorenz, Austin, Texas

I will never stop coming out and meeting people right where they are and doing the guilds. I'm trying to change that to where I can be more effective in less time. Instead of doing a one-day class and I'm just barely scratching what I can get out of that person and what's inside their soul as a quilter, in the course of a week it's amazing what they can learn.

I had quadruple heart bypass surgery in 2000. I started trying to slow down a little bit then, but it's been very little slowdown. It was a genetic problem that needed to be fixed. I was very at peace about it. I'd been very pleased with the life that I had led, and I was prepared if something went wrong in surgery that was the end of my life, and I wasn't even afraid of it. My parents were much more afraid than I was. I think my attitude helped me recover pretty good.

My life is one about variety. I'm not black-and-white; I'm gray. I ride the fence on so many issues. That's why I can quilt the Bohemian Rhapsody, which is very precise and accurate, and I'm happy making Primitive Patchwork quilts. I'm totally a Pisces. Music for me . . . Yes, I've done my classical music training; I've done the Beethoven and the Bach and the Mozart. But where I'm most happy musically—and even as a child—was creating my own music or arranging my own music.

My soul has always been about creating. Musically I love creating. I love sitting down and playing improvisationally. That is not mathematical—I mean it is, but it's not "the right answer." Beethoven's note for note for note for note is "the right answer"—miss one note, and you've played it wrong. I can leave out a note, and nobody knows, nobody cares. Quilting is probably the same way. Music and quilting to me are creative endeavors. I want to create something that gives me pleasure and gives somebody else pleasure. So if my quilts end up inspiring anybody in any way whatsoever, then I will feel that those quilts will have been a source of inspiration for them on their journey.

From a creative standpoint, it wasn't even a climb up or a climb down. It was a sidestep. I use the same things in music to create music as I'm using quilting to create the art. There's a line—a melody line. In art you create a line for the visual person to move their eye. Harmony in music creates a mood. Color in art creates a mood. So there's a parallel from side to side from those two, and I do a lecture on the topic. It's a nice sidestep for me to reach into my musical experience to express myself artistically.

I look at the cycle of life and believe in the great cosmos coming together. First of all, quilting wasn't ever going to be a part of my life—I didn't know I was ever going to quilt. All I wanted to do was make something with Granny's sewing machine. That happened to be a whole summer where I kept falling in love with it and didn't know anybody.

But the first time I met somebody who was a quilter, who actually was part of a guild and they invited me to a guild, they invited me on the second Friday night of September of 1991. I had been sewing for three months. I didn't know there was going to be a speaker. I didn't know there was a lecturer. I didn't know this existed in the world. And the speaker's name was Faye Anderson—Faye is from Boulder, Colorado. I give her tremendous credit for a lot about my life because that night she stood up and gave a lecture on the design elements of art and how they relate to quilters.

Now, I'm sitting there in the audience, never having gone to a quilt meeting in my life, and here's a lady speaking intelligently and scholarly on artistic design. And I'm sitting there for the first time in my life, going, "Wait a minute. That's exactly the same thing I do to compose music." Everything she brought out rhythm, repetition—is the same thing that's in music. It was then, that first night, that at least the seeds for formulating my own lecture on comparison between the two were born. It was born that night. I saw those parallels. Ever since the beginning, well, yeah, I'll be happy to play the piano. If I'm going to talk about music and how it relates to art, I need a piano to show these things, [so] I'll just play the piano.

And suddenly the quilters are wanting me to play something else. And so suddenly that's why these little quilt concerts/entertainment/scholarly talks, they happened on their own. I didn't set out to do that. And now it's entertainment. Instead of doing a little slide show, I've tried to put together a whole thing of comedy. I tell the whole story of Granny and Pete getting married and the sewing machine. Then I relate to quilters and their quilter stash. And me and my dad bonding because we're both guy quilters. I tell all this funny shtick that works in some scholastic information.

I have numerous programs that I give. I let them see me. I don't hide a lot about who I am, so they feel like they're really getting to know me onstage. And I'm trying to relate to them. I want them to know that I understand that we're all in this together—life. Quilting is so much more than cutting out fabrics, picking out fabrics, sewing them together. Quilting, when it comes down to it, is something that is so rich and so deep and so meaningful. We work through our greatest sorrows and the greatest joys of our lives—"Oh, someone's getting married—we gotta make them a wedding quilt. New baby's coming . . ."

The quilt becomes a landmark in life, and it also dictates and says this is where I was in my life at this time. So as a quilter, if you make a series of quilts—whether it's five or fifty in your lifetime—people, once we're gone, can just go back and chronicle our life in these sets of quilts. Whether they're utility quilts or art quilts or whatever, so much of who we are goes into that quilt. I understand that, and they understand that. That's what makes quilters so incredibly joined together. It's not like I made a series of shirts, and I go back and look at Ricky's life in a series of shirts. There's something about

I was born in Tennessee, and my grandfather gave me a beautiful Whig Rose quilt, which he bought from an elderly lady who lived up in the mountains. The appliqué and quilting were beyond description. I treasured the quilt, and it was the one thing that I had from him. I hung it on the clothesline in the garage to air it one fine day, and my husband befriended a stray dog, which he put in the garage until the owner could come and get it. The dog pulled the quilt down, chewed holes in it, and so the quilt had holes and grease all over it. You cannot imagine the trauma this created. I was hysterical.

He told me to just throw it away, and he would get me another quilt. I took the quilt, and some instinct told me to put it in a pillowcase and put it in the cedar chest. There it sat for years. However, I periodically reminded him of his grave error in judgment.

Charlie had been in the doghouse big-time all this time. We moved to Austin, and I heard of a group of ladies who quilted in Georgetown. So I took the quilt up there, and one of them said to take it home and get it as clean as possible and they could probably salvage a wall hanging out of it. We took it home and very delicately worked and got it clean, took it back up to Georgetown, and there we met Margie.

Upon hearing the story, she said to give her the quilt, [that] she would have to get him out of the doghouse. The quilt was longer in length, and so she took out a row, mended the quilt, and requilted it. I could not believe it, and I cried. And this is how Charlie got out of the doghouse. At this point in time I decided to try to quilt (I do not sew), and I became hooked on quilting.

—Nell Neunhoffer, Plano, Texas

quilting that's so much different than any of the other textile art forms. Quilting is just so rich.

I'm in Colorado now. We purchased the forty acres in southern Colorado. The desire is for it to be a place to live but also a place of growth for quilters. God forbid, I could not ever be Georgia O'Keefe, but you know what Ghost Ranch was? It was a place where she lived and artisans came, and peoples' lives were rich and they just grew because there was a place for them. If that could ever be a fraction in the quilt world of what that was for artists, it would be an incredible thing. To have a place for quilters to say, "I was there. I was in Autumn Rock. I was in this place of beauty, and my life was changed." Whether they were there for three days, five days, a week, or a month doesn't matter to me. My goal is to provide a place like that. I'm living my dream.

The bottom line is, I want people to know that I'm giving, that my desire is to give them something. And it's always been that way. When I was conducting chorale music, I wanted that choir to accomplish something that they never believed they could do or they were a part of something that they never dreamed was possible. I always wanted to give. That's why, if I'm in class or a lecture, I work really hard. It can come across as conceit or ego. It's not any of those things. It's [that] I believe in myself, I have confidence. I want them to walk away and feel like their life has been enriched. My whole life is about trying to enrich the world that we live in. You can't make yourself leave a legacy. I can care that I want to, so I just have to live my life the very best way that I can so when it's over and said and done, the legacy will be whatever it will be, because of the life I've lived.

It always feels good [to win]. When I'm in that mode of creating a quilt, knowing that it's going to be out there and it's a significant work—there's things that I do for fun, and there's things that I do [when] I want to put my best foot forward for myself, to take my own journey a little bit further, so I want to do it really well. But when I put it out there, I want it to be respected and recognized. There are too many quilts out there—a different set of judges on a different set of days and I might not have got any ribbons whatsoever. It's always exciting to win, but it's not like I was the fastest or jumped the highest. It's subjective opinions, and so I just have to thank the judges for smiling on me that day and giving me those awards. And you know, I don't know what else to say. I've received so many wonderful recognitions in the quilt world, and they're all an honor and I feel humbled by them. I feel excited about them.

7

Je Ne Sais Quilt

Lut De Meulder is in Austin for a couple of days, down from Dallas to settle her freshman son, Thomas, into his dorm for the spring semester. A Belgian-transplanted-to-France-transplanted-to-Texas (she still keeps an apartment in the South of France with her husband, Jan), Lut is an avid quilter who took up the art the first time she lived in the States, back in 1990. Sarah and her daughter, Emma, and our friend Ann and I meet up with Lut and Thomas at Chez Nous, a little French bistro downtown, to share dinner and quilting anecdotes.

I pull out my "masterpiece"—the comforter top I'm so slowly working on, the one with the abundance of yellow and purple "filler" squares—and Lut praises me. I've seen pictures of Lut's work, the detail, the perfection, and recognize the generosity of her praise. She's cutting me a lot slack, the way a wise teacher might encourage the simple line drawings of an eager child. In fact, although she isn't my teacher, she does teach quilting—and whether her patience led her down the teaching path or vice versa, it's good to be on the receiving end of her compliments.

Lut chose quilting as a means of acclimation. "When I moved here, I wanted to learn through the quilt some of the American history," she says. She quickly found more than history lessons in her pursuit of quilting. "I met the most wonderful sharing and caring women you can imagine."

Consulting with her son and the waiter to find the right words in English, she explains to us how every big city has a welcoming center for immigrants. Now when a Frenchwoman moves to Dallas and investigates what the French community there is offering, she has a chance to sign up for one of Lut's classes.

Official quilting guilds, informal gatherings, and good old-fashioned quilting bees have always been about more than sewing. To be certain, tips on fabrics and stitching techniques are a mainstay of such rendezvous, but of course there will always be the delightful straying from topic—conversational tangents being another given and part of the appeal of quilting with others.

For Lut's students, there are added benefits. "We discuss current events in the news and what's going on in Dallas," Lut says. "A lot of these women don't speak enough English to get involved with their local life. I often tell them what movie was good, stuff like that."

They also get two sets of lessons for the price of one. "Most of them never held a needle," Lut points out. "If they do a certain pattern, I explain where it came from. Simply the expression 'log cabin'—they don't know what it is. So I explain what a log cabin is." And then she explains the significance of the pattern that has the same name as the pioneer house, sharing with them the history of the Underground Railroad and using this to segue into other American history lessons. "Quilts call forth a very specific sense of American strength and can-do," she says. "Quilting is an American pastime that honors a tradition of women more than making do with what little they had. It honors taking scraps and making something useful and artful."

At dinner, we immerse ourselves in French bread and quilting tales. Sarah produces the pretty blue quilt top she's been working on with the odd geometric shapes. Lut exclaims, "It's so you!" And it is.

We discuss styles and techniques, and Lut admits she is no fan of "message quilts" that often have long explanations printed up on nearby placards to help viewers understand them. "If I have to read a whole page to understand it, I don't like that," she says. "I remember in Houston years ago one woman said,

---

My best quilting advice I heard from Ami Simms: "If this is not the last quilt you will ever make, give yourself a break." The only quilting advice I'd like to share is let your intuition and imagination go free.

—Shelly Sutton, Cedar Park, Texas

'I've been going through therapy for so many years—I finally I discovered what is wrong with me. I was sexually touched when I was a kid. So to get rid of all my anger, I made this quilt.' And it was like a three-yard vagina!"

Thomas, perhaps shy to be at a table full of women or perhaps just eager to get back to his friends in the dorm, is more reticent. Asked how many quilts his mother has made, he just laughs. Together the two of them describe the quilt she's sent him off to school with—pieced together with trademarked Coca-Cola fabric in honor of Thomas's favorite beverage.

When I mention my trepidation at the task before me—how will I ever be even one-tenth as good at quilting as my friends?—Lut reminds me what the Amish quilters say: "Only God is flawless." And so they put purposeful mistakes in their quilts to avoid being perfect. (I respond that then, given my first project, I should be granted instant honorary Amish-hood.)

Thanks in great part to my ongoing exploration of quilting—and my fun if totally inaccurate "theory" that if I just talk about quilting long enough with enough quilters, I'll be able to skip all that learning stuff and become a quilter by osmosis—my friendship with Lut grows and thrives.

A couple of years into my undercover adventure, after a number of meals at Chez Nous and one particularly memorable breakfast at Denny's where Lut soothed a very distraught me, promising me I really would figure out quilting—this pep talk occurring during that self-pitying phase when I wanted Sarah to be teaching me twenty-four hours a day and Sarah didn't have the time—I hopped in my car and drove to Dallas to meet Lut's French quilting group and her American quilting group and to attend a meeting of the Quilters Guild of Plano. (I knew a little about this guild—Lut had given me the QGP cookbook for my birthday one year, and I was especially fond of a crab-and-spinach dip recipe in it called Astroturf.)

Let's just say, when it comes to taste, Lut and I are at the opposite ends of the spectrum. Me? I have No Taste. Lut, on the other hand, has a gorgeous house filled with treasures from around the world. Even her quilting friends—three Frenchwomen—are stylishly dressed.

I take my place at the dining room table. There is a beautiful tapestry on the wall behind me. In front of me the women sit, patiently cutting out tiny Christmas shapes from fabric to be appliquéd onto a quilt wall hanging. Between Lut's fluent English, the limited but nonetheless impressive English of her friends, and my wild gesticulating (since I don't know any French), we manage to have a great conversation. This is not your archetypal old-ladies-at-church quilting bee. We discuss politics and culture and parenting and, yes, even quilting(apparently there is one very expensive quilt shop in Paris). Before meeting Lut, none of these women ever quilted. Now they love it.

We break for lunch, at which point members of Lut's American quilt group join us for a lunch of salmon quiche, a salad of grapes and greens and cubes of bleu cheese, fresh baguettes, and (scandalous!) wine. Heavy Texas accents mix with heavy French accents. Lut shows off her quilted place mats from the South of France, and this launches us into a discussion of utilitarian quilting—table quilts, bedspreads. "The worst quilt in the world will keep you warm," one of the Americans points out. I decide that eating piles of French food and talking about quilting is a new favorite combination of mine.

We have a faux debate over whether or not we should have dessert, and then, of course, we all have dessert. This is followed up by show-and-tell. Today the Americans have brought along their favorite quilts to show to the Frenchwomen. First Bev shows her quilts to us, and everyone oohs and ahhs. Then Frances shows her quilts and everyone oohs and aahs. Not one single ooh or aah is gratuitous. This work is truly impressive.

After lunch, the ladies pack up and leave, and Lut gives me a tour of her quilts, which are located all throughout her expansive home. Lut likes traditional patterns and appliqué, and she likes holiday quilts. It seems she's got one made for every occasion. Above her fireplace is an appliquéd quilt called The Tree of Life, and the details are meticulous and amazing. Lut smiles as I scrutinize, trying to comprehend how someone could make such a thing. "That's the one my kids will be fighting over when I die," she says.

My gaze wanders from the quilt to Lut's stash, which is large and organized by color in some built-in shelves near her sewing area. She's also got a quilting frame set up. She settles in to do some sewing and I plop down on a nearby couch to watch some Dr. Phil, and we chat as she works, swapping talk about quilting and the complicated lives of Dr. Phil's guests.

After dinner with Lut's husband, Jan, Lut and I drive over to a big church for the meeting of the Quilters Guild of Plano. The group is boisterous and joyful, the corridor filled with a loud and happy hum as the quilters greet each other. As we sign in, we're invited to take a survey, for which we are rewarded with a homemade pot holder—made with loops on one of those little plastic looms.

My new potholder triggers very happy memories for me of childhood crafts. And it connects me to the present too. I don't think I know anyone who doesn't like making things. The joy of arts and crafts visits us when we're little, and it never lets go. I remember one time when my son was little, and my friend Lenny, a lawyer, dropped by in the afternoon on a break from his high-stress job. Absentmindedly he picked up some Play-Doh and started playing. He immediately relaxed and, before leaving, suggested that I consider opening a day care center for overworked adults who could use a little bit of crafting to lighten their load.

Surely, then, for many quilters there is a similar connection between quilting and childhood fun. Which is not to say that quilting is simplistic, as easy to master as a little loop pot holder. Of course it's not. Obviously quilting can be deeply complex and intensely intricate. But that feeling—"Yippee! I'm making stuff with my hands!"—must be one of the biggest reasons that quilting is so appealing and ultimately satisfying for so many people.

Having never attended a guild meeting before, I'm surprised at how many quilters are packed into the room. The place is abuzz with excitement. A speaker is lined up to tell the group about her specialty, a certain type of appliqué. She hovers in the back of the room, her big Texas hair and liberally applied, brightly colored makeup giving her a surreal quality. But first there are announcements. We've got the block of the month to discuss and a request for quilts for four children in a family where the father has suddenly died. And then, after the announcement but before the speaker, we have door prizes!

Door prizes—the prospect of winning them, that is—are like loopy pot holders to me. I get very excited with anticipation. I time-trip back to little treats won in elementary school and at festive events. Though intellectually I know my odds of winning are slim and that the numbers have already been pulled from the hat, I still tell myself if I just wish hard enough, my number will be called.

This night, at the end of a day full of nothing but quilting happiness, my wish comes true. First, Lut's number gets called. I hardly have time to be jealous before my own number gets called. I open up my little paper bag—a ten-dollar gift certificate from a local quilting store. The feeling of winning is enough for me, and besides, I'm heading back to Austin. I hand over the certificate to my friend—a small token of gratitude for all she's taught me about quilting.

8

Another Kind of Quilting Cotton

Joann Czenze Cotton is a friend of my oldest sister, Dolly. When I told Dolly about writing this book, she insisted I meet Joann, who had made quilts for Dolly's kids. These quilts are already family treasures, made of blocks contributed by various family members and blocks featuring photos of the kids on special occasions.

Joann doesn't make the sort of quilts you enter in shows. Joann's specialty is making quilts that bring comfort. And not just to her family and my family. Years ago, when the AIDS epidemic was first spreading, Joann had an experience that changed her forever and influenced a quilting project that is well into its second decade now.

" I was sewing since I was young. I love sewing. My problem is I don't have enough time. Or I get started and get into it and I'll stay up until two, three in the morning. And I can't do that. 'Cause I need sleep.

The first quilt I made was a gift, a baby quilt. I can tell you exactly—it was gingham and Swiss dots. And I cut out squares and I put them together—yellow, blue, green, pink. It was a gift for someone I worked with, and it was her first baby.

So that's how I started. Then I really didn't do that much. I think I made maybe three more baby quilts like that. I just did that, and that was it. And I hadn't done anything for about ten years.

And then I went through the "blind period." I worked as a nurse, and that blind period was when we didn't know anything about AIDS. You didn't wear gloves; you didn't protect yourself. I mean, there were times I'd be in ER or the ICU and we'd get all bloody, and it was okay.

You would clean up, and that was it. But you didn't have scrubs on. You just kind of poured hydrogen peroxide on it and got the worst off and worked. So I do have a lot of coworkers I lost [to AIDS].

A group of women at my church started making the quilts for AIDS [victims]. And that's why I do it, to remember—my way of saying thanks that I survived that period.

Joann takes me to her church, St. Bartholomew's, in Cherry Hill, New Jersey, to show me where her group meets to quilt. In a hallway hangs another quilt she worked on to commemorate a different tragedy.

" When September 11 happened, all the kids were really pretty upset, and we did make care packages to send up there. I really felt that the kids needed something else, and so what I did was, I had the kids from the church make the squares and I put it together. We had the squares, and they sat at the table and they drew their own picture. I thought that this was one way that they'd never forget that this happened in their tender years and that out of this there can be a lot of growth. The littlest [quilter] was eighteen months old. I think the oldest one was fourteen.

There's a group of us that gets together once a month. We meet once a month for about two and a half hours and we solve the world's problems, and we get quilts done. They're adult single size and infant size.

This is the room where we meet once a month. All this fabric has been

It is right if it is right to you whether or not you did it the way every one else did it. Take all the help and advice given, but do not let anyone tell you, you cannot do it. —Oma Harlan, Austin, Texas

donated. There are maybe five or six of us that meet. Most are not even from this church. They're friends of mine—they just come out.

When the quilts are finished, we give them to Project Linus. [There's] a woman who collects all these quilts, and she passes them out to long-term care facilities, kids with AIDS, kids on chemo, that type of thing.

I was pregnant with my eighteen-year-old daughter when I started this. A lot of the people have left, but I've kept it going only because it's my way of saying thanks for going through that blind period. We don't even know how many we've made, because we never really kept track of it.

We make about fifty or sixty a year. We've got an assembly line going. I was very much a traditionalist [when I started]—everything had to match. There was someone here who told me anything goes, and I was able to let go. [Joann points to a particular quilt.] I would never think of putting this together before, you know, because I would say you can't put ice cream cones with hearts, and yet it works.

We're using a serger to put them together. It goes really fast. I have two women who come, and all they do is tie. We used to have labels that said "Especially Made for You by St. Bartholomew's Church." These are the labels I used to buy. They're just so expensive. I think it was about twenty-five dollars for fifty. You know, when I can get them free from Project Linus, I may as well get them from there and put that difference into the supplies.

My thinking is, is, I want to present something to someone who doesn't have anything, something that I would be willing to use. Because I feel I'm doing no justice to them, I'm showing them no respect. I'm showing them nothing unless I give them something of the same quality that I would want.

I make sure that they all get blessed before they go. We have a service on Sunday, and they're all laid out on the altar railing and they all get blessed. That's very important to us. Plus the congregation gets to see what just a few people can do. And it's interesting because parishioners go up there, and there [the quilts] are on the railing. And they'll have their hands out for the communion, and you can see them feeling the quilts. So it's not just us; it's us as a community. It's one way of showing we can do small things and help. It's not something that you have to put your whole life on the side and say, "Okay, this is it. I'm going to do this."

9

Give Us This Day Our Dailey Thread

When my son, Henry, was in seventh grade at Kealing Junior High School in Austin, he had the great fortune of scoring Ms. Renée Dailey for a history teacher. Unlike some teachers, Ms. Dailey wasn't excessive with the homework. Nor did she believe in being tough as a means of educating kids. What she lacked in the ways of drill sergeant, she easily made up for with her nurturing. Henry could not get enough of her class and her personality. Every day he'd tell me, "Ms. Dailey did this!" or "Ms. Dailey did that!" Ms. Dailey brought snacks, told stories, doted on the kids. I have no doubt that for the rest of his life, when Henry looks back, Ms. Dailey will always easily be a standout on his Top Ten Favorite Teachers of All Time list.

One thing that impresses me about Ms. Dailey is a particularly ambitious project she has undertaken each spring with her kids since she started teaching nearly thirty years ago. As part of a history unit, she teaches each and every one of them to make a miniature quilt. The kids may not bring in precut fabric. They have to do every bit of the cutting and stitching themselves (well, okay, sometimes they do get assistance, but only from Ms. Dailey herself). They work diligently and on deadline, which is

how, no kidding, my son managed to finish his first quilt long before I finished mine. I've got it hanging on my bedroom wall—that little quilt is
one of my true treasures.

I visited Ms. Dailey after school one day in her classroom to talk about
this ongoing project of hers. We sat in those uncomfortable one-piece
desk/chair units that kids have to sit in all day, but Ms. Dailey, dressed to
the nines, made me feel like I was sitting in her living room on a plush
couch on a Sunday morning. She has a way of putting folks at ease immediately, and she is not shy. When I asked her to tell me how quilting became such a big part of her life, she launched right into the tale, starting
at the beginning, over four decades ago:

❝ My first experience with quilting—I guess sewing, period—would be with
my mom. My mom was a stay-at-home mom. And my mom did lots of things
with us—we crocheted, we sewed, we made dolls' clothes, we made rag dolls,
we did wood carvings. Just anything that my mom could come up with for us
to do, we did. And not only did we do it, but all of the kids in the neighborhood did too.

We had a large screened porch, which was a wraparound porch, in Louisiana. My mom would have all of us in the summertime, and my mom was the
only mom who was home all day. So in the summertime after kids had breakfast—a lot of them had breakfast at our house—they would come up, and as
soon as they gathered on the porch, my mom would start her day, taking out
paper that she had precut on pieces of wood or fabric. One of the things she
taught us how to do was to make yo-yos. It's a little round piece of fabric, and
you gather it and you pull it and it makes a cute little circle, and you piece
them all together to make a quilt top.

She got us in the habit of making the little yo-yos that she would later use
to make her quilt tops. So we were actually getting her work done for her.
Sometimes we would cut squares or rectangles—I call it the dirty work of
quilting. And the kids [Ms. Dailey's students] call it the dirty work too, because it's what they like least. But I tell them to design their quilt . . . they
don't like to do that. They feel like they should just have it cut and it should
already be going.

Every year at least one child will come with a bag of the precut pieces, and
I'll say, "You can't do that," because I try to teach across the curriculum with

it—we do the writing part, we do the math part. So then they have to back up, and that's why they think it's the dirty work. It maybe takes out a little bit of the fun, but the spark comes back right away after they're done with that part.

With my mom, we would work with the kids, and then in the evenings, after everything would be done, my mom would pull out her quilting. And we had a room, her sewing room. She had large tables around the walls. She had her sewing machine, a little black Singer sewing machine where she would sit and stitch. She did a lot of her quilting by hand—that was her choice. She always pieced the top by hand.

The actual quilting she might do on the machine, or she did it with a series of knots. Sometimes she left them where they were visible and sometimes after she did that she would put a button through. We had a button box—everybody contributed to the button box. My mom would actually take clothing apart that we no longer used or had outgrown. And she could've easily bought the fabric, but she said, "That's a waste."

So she would take it apart and she would smooth it out, because it had already been washed, and she would fold it up and usually put it in little bundles by color or by design. She might have all of the plaids here or a layer of plaids and a layer of solid colors.

My mom had a quilt she called *Some of Everybody*. It had things on it that belonged to my grandmother Virginia, to my grandma Dora, my grandfather, and to Willy Dailey. I remember my favorite piece on that quilt was, my brother had a little white shirt that had red and blue lighthouses on it. And what she would do, after she got them in there, she would embroider. She might put on their name, and she would put the year. She would put bits of information on to them, and we would get them and we knew. We'd say, "This was Grandma's dress," because there was piece in there with a navy blue that had white polka dots on it. And I would say, "This is Grandma Ginny's dress."

The only precut pieces I ever saw my mom use . . . My dad used to, in his spare time, he tailored suits, and he had all of these little wool samples. And when the samples would no longer be offered, then my mom put them into a quilt top, and it just grew and it grew and it grew. My mom was making king-size quilts before king-size beds.

She got your quilt on your bed with the first cold front. My mom would've had everything out on the line soaking up the sun, getting them fresh. And she would've brought them in, and everybody would've gotten a quilt on their bed.

In the wintertime the quilts rotated. My mom might say, "I'm going to put this quilt on your bed this week because your brother's kicking is tearing up my quilt." My brother would roll up in the wintertime—he would actually put it on the bed and he rolled up in it and he would flip himself over on his face. My mom would always say, "He's tearing up my quilts. When I have to work with your brother's quilts, it's almost like making a quilt all over again."

Another thing that came up this summer when we were looking at some quilts, my mom said, "I want to show you something." And she got out this quilt, and it had a little pattern in it—looks like an apple blossom but it was on, like, a sea foam background. She said, "Remember this?" And I said, "Yes, that was a skirt you made me." She said, "Let me show you something." And she went in her bedroom, and she came back out and she said, "I got this at the fabric store last week." A lot of the old fabrics are coming back again. It might not even be cotton. It may be coming out as a print on some of the spandex. But they're pulling those old dye lots out and all of that stuff, and they're using it again.

But she would've put them on our beds, and we would've talked about the quilts and, you know, "I made this" and "I did this" and "Do you remember this?" and "Do you know who this belonged to?" There's a quilt my mom has, and it has an old piece of my dad's army jacket. But it's wool. That old green ugly-looking wool like blankets used to be made of—there's a piece of that in it. You can almost mark time with them. She has a quilt that is made almost totally and completely of polyester pieces. So you know they mark different eras with the polyester.

I tell the kids, I always say, "Now, you know what? Don't bring anything that stretches. It's too hard to work with," because they run into problems. But my mom worked with that stuff because she was good at that.

I like making quilts, but I like making tiny little quilts, little mini-quilts. I

It's about the only thing my late mother and I ever got along doing without major fights. We would spot a fabric store, and one of us would start to say, "Oh, I need. . ." And suddenly we'd both look at each other and chant, "Need has nothing to do with it!" — Kelly Wagner, Austin, Texas

make them, and I give them to the people at my church. I've never made anything that I've kept. I give it away. Even the little demo quilt that I do with the kids when we're doing the unit, I end up giving it to somebody.

In '77, my first teaching experience, I made quilts with the kids in the class that I had. What ended up happening, I started just collecting stuff, and now I have this big fat notebook that I do my quilting unit from. It used to be purely a February thing for me, for Black History Month. With them, I would tell them about the message in the quilt and the many uses of a quilt. Then I took it all the way back—the first quilts were used as floor coverings. It was warm, and it was done in Asia. They made quilts.

A quilt is a sandwich. That's what I always tell the kids. That's how I introduce it: "If you want to make a mental picture, it's a sandwich. You have two slices of bread and a filler, and that's actually the top, the bottom, and the insulation. The insulation is your batting." And then I tell them [that] when quilts were made, if you were not real wealthy—if you could find a really old quilt that was maybe made by a sharecropper family—instead of having the nice neat batting in it, it would actually have pieces of clothing. Or maybe they would just fold it and overlap it for the center, and the better pieces would go on top, usually feed sacks or flour sacks on top. And it had very little piecework to it because they didn't have time to sit and do piecework.

If you looked at some of the quilts made in the New England colonies, even though they were made by slaves, they were very elaborate quilts because they were made with the finest fabric and the best insulation. They were more for show than anything else, even though they might've served a practical purpose. Quilts were also a way of flaunting your wealth—the more intricate quilts—because there would be very little patchwork, and the piecework would be more geometric, and that piecework would still be less than the appliqué. It was more like a piece of art. You had your very best, and I always tell the kids [that] if you had guests who were coming to stay for a while, you made sure you put the best quilt you had in the room where they stayed.

At this age a lot of things surprise them. This is what comes up most of the time: "So the Underground Railroad wasn't really underground?"

I start out with some piecework, and I stand at the door for a whole week before I even mention it. So for a whole week they're seeing me working on something, and it grows and I never make a big deal out of it. Somebody will inevitably say, every period, "Can I try that?" and I say, "No, you wouldn't be interested." Or I'll say things like, "It looks like it's fun, but it's hard work. This is hard work. You wouldn't want to do it. You're not going to be interested in this." And I'll let it grow and let it grow, and by the end of the week somebody wants to know, "Are we going to get to do that?" I say, "Yeah, maybe."

I usually have one class that I'll just let start it and let them run away with it before I pull the other kids in. Now it's gotten to the point where they show up at the beginning of the year: "Are we going to make quilts in here?"

Once I get them started, I cut out hand towels, and I say, "Your tools you're going to need tomorrow will be your needle and thread and a ruler." And I make them measure several inches on a sheet of paper. And [I] say, "What I want you to do is just stitch the line." And I teach them the running stitch, and I tell them to draw a three-inch line on the paper. I teach them how to knot the thread and stitch the paper. And then I say, "Now, this is what I want you to do. I want you to measure an inch, and every time you see a stitch, tell me how many stitches you got to that inch." And they'll say, "Hmm, I got three." "I only got two." We talk about the strength of that, and I'll tell them expert quilters are capable of getting nine to twelve stitches to an inch. Some of them can even get sixteen stitches to an inch. But I say, you know what? This is a situation where more is not always better, because usually when you pass the twelve-to-sixteen mark, it will rip the fabric and it's no longer sturdy, so more is not better in this case.

I say, "I always kind of hate this, but the boys are going to have the best quilts." And they do. Because of the gender thing. They don't want to be laughed at; they don't want to be made fun of. And they take it more seriously than the girls do. I mean, they come to stay after school. They will call you at your house: "Hi, Ms. Dailey. This is Pat. I just needed to know . . ." or "Ms. Dailey, this is so-and-so's mom, and we have just had a horrible evening here. The quilt didn't come out, and he tore it up."

The boys by far have the most intricate patterns, the best stitching, the most creativity, the best projects. This is something else that happens with the boys—I tell them minimum size is twelve by twelve, the size of one of these floor tiles, but if you feel super-ambitious, you can make it as big at you like. The boys will always have one that's larger.

We paper-quilt first—you have to draw it on paper. Very few kids end up with what they drew on paper. They have to modify. You know, on paper you can be real ambitious—"I'm going to do this, and I'm going to do this." What usually happens—the great quilts are the ones where you have kids who figure out "I want different textures in mine" or "I'm going to do all three," because I introduce patchwork and then I do tell them about appliqué and crazy quilting. And you'll get one where a kid will say, "I'm putting everything on mine." I'll say, "Well, how're you going to do that?"

I had a kid last year, and he is so meticulous and he is so perfect. He would stitch, and he would rip. He would just get furious. And I would watch him, and he would cuss and cuss at the quilt, and I would hear it and I would ig-

---

Like many quilters, once I started, I became obsessed with fabric and patterns. I'm the world's most impatient person, but when it comes to quilting and designing, I can work ten to twelve hours a day and stop only to go to the toilet and to eat. I go to the gym early in the morning to strengthen my muscles so I don't get back pain while working all day.

What fascinates me are the design possibilities, and while I'm working on one quilt, I start two or three others. I can't wait to finish so I can begin the next one. I wish I had an assistant to finish my projects and to clean up my mess, because once I get an idea, I go through my fabric stash like a whirlwind to find what I'm looking for. Like many quilting fanatics, I buy fabric first and store it (sometimes for years) and then create the projects. In other words, the fabric dictates what I will do.

I've been told that the Amish quilters always included a "spirit door" in their quilts. This means they purposefully include a mistake—a misplaced triangle, an upside-down design, etc. Why? I've been told that they believe only God is perfect and therefore they need to show their imperfections. Well, often I find that I have made an error in my piecing that is not always noticeable to the viewer. In fact, I don't discover the error until I take a picture of the quilt or look at it from a great distance. So when this happens, I call it my spirit door.

That's the neat thing. There are no mistakes. When things don't go as I plan, or if I accidentally cut into the finished project, I treat that as a learning experience and change the quilt by adding or deleting. I make it work. Often the "mistakes" make the most wonderful quilts—a total surprise.

—Sara Castle, Del Rio, Texas

---

nore it. And I said, "You know, it's really not hard to do. Give me all of your pieces." And I sat and I put together a pretty good piece, and I said, "Look at how good that looks," and it just made him work with it. He got another piece connected and another piece, and he was so proud of it. He said, "Look, look! I got it going. Can I take it home?" I said, "Take it home—do whatever you need to do with it." And he came back with it finished.

I'll tell you [about] another kid who had a terrible time with it, but once he caught on, Jerry had a quilt that had about a hundred and forty-four pieces in it, and those hundred and forty-four pieces put together are a twelve-by-twelve square. It was black and white, and what kicked his butt with it [was that] the white pieces were cut out of a T-shirt. He cried, he would ball it up. Now, he never tore it up—he had enough sense not to tear it up. He would ball it up and stuff it in the bag. He'd throw it.

But once he got it going, he would run in here, go to the box, get it out, and he'd be just going away. He'd push his hair back out of his eyes and he'd go. I can remember the day he finally got the top finished; then he got laid-back with it. I almost had to talk about calling his dad to make him finish. He was like, "I'm almost through with it." He just got so comfortable with it. He did finish it, and it was a job well done. He had a hundred and forty-four pieces in that finished twelve-by-twelve, and I kept on saying, "Don't bite off a hunk bigger than you can chew." But he knew he could do it.

I like doing it with the kids because they form camaraderie, and I'm real big on cooperative education. They learn how to help. It makes them think. It makes them creative. You'll hear kids say to other kids, "Oh, I wish I had seen that fabric," and the other kid will say, "Why don't we mix them? If you give me this much of that, I'll give you this much of my piece, and then we can put them together." And you can see their minds working.

What they like to do when we're done . . . I lay all of the quilts out, and they'll say, "Oh, I bet that belongs to Henry, because I gave him that piece of fabric right there." And they'll say, "She gave me this." Or they'll look and say, "I never even thought about doing that. Can we make another one?" Many times, after the project is over, kids will come after school and say, "You going to be here today? I'm going to work on this quilt I'm making." Somebody came by last year and said, "Do you know I made another quilt? And I gave it to a lady at my church who was having a baby." I enjoy seeing them do it. I enjoy seeing how creative they can actually be. I like the way it settles them down.

10

Meet My Famous Mother
. . . er . . . Daughter

Marti and Stacy Michell are mother and daughter. Both are famous in the quilting world. Marti is famous in the United States for her quilting and her quilting techniques—in the late sixties and early seventies she helped push forward the new wave of quilting that had surfaced. Back then Stacy was a little kid, but not too little to be involved. She and her brother helped Marti put together quilting kits for people who ordered from all over the country. Growing up in the quilting world, she often found herself referred to as "Marti's daughter."

Meanwhile, over in Japan, Stacy is the famous one and Marti is known as "Stacy's mother." Quilting is extremely popular in Japan, and many quilters are in love with Stacy's hand-dyed fabrics, which she makes at her studio in Marietta, Georgia. She's so well loved, in fact, that one client ordered a bolt of every single color Stacy dyes. These bolts were placed in a small private museum where only a privileged few get the opportunity to sit and observe them. Her fabric is also a favorite of Kathy Nakajima, who is sort of the Martha Stewart of Japan. Kathy won Best of Show at IQF 2003 with a quilt she made using Stacy's fabric.

I met both women for the first time at IQF 2003. The way I remember it, I stumbled into Stacy's little booth. I was probably in search of her mother because, no doubt, someone had suggested her as a good interview subject. Marti, who always has a booth adjacent to Stacy's at IQF, was off teaching a class, though. Stacy greeted me warmly and enthusiastically. In fact, she was so enthusiastic, I thought surely this must be an act. Once again, as I had been so many times before in my quest to understand quilting and quilters, I was entirely wrong.

Stacy, I now know, is almost always enthusiastic. I say "almost always" because I admit I have not seen her jet-lagged after one of her whirlwind Atlanta-to-Houston-to-Yokohama-back-to-Atlanta trips in the fall. Surely this must slow her down. Or maybe not.

Marti, likewise, is high-energy and ever ready with a smile. When I first met her, tracking her down a few hours after meeting Stacy, I did a double take—the two women look remarkably alike. I interviewed them both that year. At IQF 2004, Marti was too busy to talk—she'd been selected as the honoree for the Silver Star Award, which commemorates a lifetime of achievements in the quilting world.

Stacy did make time for me. Lots of it. We took the escalator up to the pressroom and plopped down and talked. And talked and talked and talked. Stacy described quilt week in Yokohama, Japan, where she was heading as soon as the Houston show finished. She told me how, on opening day, she gets a little embarrassed because so many Japanese quilters push their way into her tiny stall to buy up all her fabrics while other, nearby vendors stand by, idle in their own booths, and watch the mad rush. And she told me about her big plans for the immediate future—her trip to Japan, which meant "twelve days, two climates, one suitcase, absolutely nothing extra"—and her bigger plans for the slightly less immediate future.

Here are the tales of mother and daughter:

MARTI MICHELL

"I'm a sewer first. I was teaching sewing classes at home because at that time Stacy was a little girl and I wanted to be home more. I was a textiles and clothing and journalism major at Iowa State [double major], so I was teaching set-in sleeves and buttonholes and playing around and doing patchwork. Actually it was because of a little dress I made for Stacy. I had done her whole little

Mother and daughter quilting stars Stacy and Marti Michell. In the United States,
Stacy is often referred to in the quilting world as "Marti's daughter."
In Japan, Marti is better known as "Stacy's mother." Photo courtesy of Stacy Michell.

summer wardrobe of shirts and shorts and stuff, and I had taken all of the coordinated fabrics and made patchwork fabric and then cut her a little prairie dress. It was the little patchwork dress that really got me hooked. Then the students caught on and thought it would be a whole lot more fun to do patchwork—"Teach us that! Teach us that!"—so I started doing quilting classes.

There were virtually no books. We were doing self-taught things. Then we started making kits because cotton fabric was hard to find—hard to believe now. I would find cotton fabric and put it into kits for my students. Then the students wanted more and their friends wanted some, and we ended up with a patchwork kit company.

There *was* fabric—it was just hard to find. Each store would have a little, so I would go everywhere. I was buying retail to begin with and then just cutting up kits for my students.

We're in Atlanta. We don't have a shop. We are manufacturers. The company [that had the kits]—we did publishing and all kinds of things—was sold in 1985. From '85 to '95, I did all kinds of freelance—fabric design, book writing, and patterns for McCall's, and designing of tools for other companies.

Then around '95 somebody asked us to develop this template line, acrylic templates for rotary cutting. So right now we're manufacturers of that—specialty rulers.

We're just a company like everybody else. I've done a lot of guest appearances on TV shows. I just finished four years as president of the International Quilt Association. It's a volunteer job. Just because I've been around so long. My husband and I do an event with Quilt Market on a freelance basis for Karey so that shop owners all know us because of that event. We're just real well-known.

I've had, historically, one of the best-selling books, *Quilting for People Who Don't Have Time to Quilt*—450,000 copies sold. I've had fabric designs that have been multimillion-yard sellers. The first thirteen fabrics I did, six of them were over a million-yard sellers. Historically, they call me a pioneer in this quilt revival.

If I had more free time, I would quilt. It's just fun. It's creative. I love sewing. I love fabrics, and I love putting them together.

Stacy has a very different thing, a different approach. It's fun when we can do things together—like this quilt is her fabric, my templates. Every now and then we get to travel together and do shows in Japan.

STACY MICHELL

" I own Shades Textiles out of Marietta, Georgia. In 1986, I exhibited here at Quilt Market and Quilt Festival for the first time, and I sold to a Japanese man that was Kathy [Nakajima]'s teacher. For the past seventeen years, I've been shipping fabric to Japan, and Kathy buys and uses a lot of it. I have two books of hers in my booth, one of which is almost exclusively my fabric. She has published thirty-one books in Japan—ten of them on quilting.

I've been to Japan seven times now, and I'm going back November 15 for Quilt Week Yokohama. I'm going back in January for the Tokyo quilt show. For me it's even more complicated and convoluted sometimes. My mother is Marti Michell, [now former] president of IQA and a very famous American quilter. So for seventeen years now, I've had my business. But in the States, Marti's so famous it's hard for me to be anyone other than Marti's daughter. It's nice sometimes when I meet people who don't know the correlation.

In Japan it's not just the language that's different; the techniques are different. Japanese quilters are much more likely to do everything by hand and with scissors. And Marti promotes rotary cutters and sewing machines, so in Japan they really don't know who Marti is. But I've had this huge marketplace in Japan for all these years now, so when I travel to Japan, she's Stacy's mother.

I do quilt, though not as much as I'd like to. I was given a Singer Featherweight for Christmas when I was six years old. I didn't get the plastic one that my friend Tammy got. I traded it back to my mom for a Pfaff about fifteen years ago. It's still in the family. I sewed all through elementary school.

She used to have a different company in the quilting business, and that was the only job I ever had before I completed my college education and started my business. So I started out about twenty-one years old with this business and have just continued with it ever since. One of the best parts of this job is being able to travel the world.

Many years ago I started selling fabric to a lot of the Japanese quilters, and they started breaking the rules of Hawaiian quilts, which are usually two solid colors, and they started putting my hand-dyed fabrics in them. Sky fabrics in the background, different colored fabrics on top. I looked at that and said, "You know, somebody needs to break the rules of Hawaiian designs being Hawaiian." So we came out with this whole line of patterns that we call All-Around Appliqué Designs. They're on any theme but Hawaiian. So they're things like All-Around the Baby's Room, All-Around the Kitchen, All-Around the Golf Course, but they still the use the fold-it, cut-it, open-it style of Hawaiian appliqué. So then that inspired new fabric. So this fabric—we call it "color block cloth," and it's dyed in specific ways to align with the two layers of the appliqué.

I dyed about two hundred of one particular size before I left for Tokyo in 2002. I came home with twenty. Well, it's after the show that I have time to do my projects, right? And what am I left with? The twenty pieces that nobody wanted. So I had this piece and the reverse of this piece, which meant it was black with four yellow blotches on it. They were pretty ugly, okay? And so I double-challenged myself in the bad department. I said, "What's the worst-selling appliqué pattern? If I'm going to get left with the worst-selling fabric, let's use the worst-selling appliqué pattern, and that happens to be All-Around the Pond. So I chose two of the designs from All-Around the Pond and made this piece, which I think is really cool. So this is a piece of the large color block cloth with four focal points. I left the background whole, cut the foreground into four pieces, cut the appliqué out of the four pieces, and positioned those on the front.

I only have a studio in Atlanta, a loft space in a big old furniture factory with a lot of artists. I'm out selling about 25 to 30 percent of the year. I do Paducah. I do Quilt Hawaii and meet the Japanese customers in Hawaii in the summer. I've got about three people working in the studio on a pretty steady basis and then a couple of other people that I call on from time to time.

One year here in Houston, I guess eleven years ago, I brought a woman that worked with me in the studio, and we'd been working together forty to fifty hours a week. And then we got to Houston, and I fired her while we were there. It was really miserable—we were still sharing a hotel room and sitting next to each other on the plane on the way home—and I said, "No more studio people traveling with me. It's too much togetherness."

I have the coolest job in the world. I've worked hard for it. We have a new venture in Atlanta. My adjacent studio came available. I've been there twelve years. I have a thirty-six hundred square foot studio now. After the expansion, we'll have about six thousand square feet. And so I'm getting a new living space [in the loft], because my living quarters have gotten smaller and smaller.

I'm thinking about the next ten years of the career. The next ten years are going to be more quilting teaching and such, more of the personality business. I figure, why not?

I'm expanding. It has it's own title: the Quilt Spa and Finishing School. We're going to have classes.

Japanese quilting school is a lot different than American, and I'm thinking of incorporating some of that. [In] Japanese quilting school you sign up for a four-year program, and you're a master quilter at the end of that. There's a much bigger curriculum. Maybe you know things coming into the class, but you're going to start over at this teacher's step one. I'm thinking about having that approach, in part because then I could affiliate my school with the university system.

11

Reaping What They Sew

By the time I got to IQF 2004, I was hardly an expert—and I still had not finished my first first quilt, that biggish scrapaholic masterpiece I'd begun seventeen months prior—but I did know a few things. I understood some of the terminology now and how it translated to the quilts: appliquéd, hand quilted, machine quilted, hand-dyed fabrics, pieced, whole cloth.

Better still, I felt something bordering on confidence as I walked into the convention center. I knew what to expect, as much as one can know what to expect when stepping into a huge space with nearly two thousand pieces of art I'd never seen before and hundreds of vendors. I also knew, to a certain extent, *who* to expect.

By now, two years into thinking about quilts, and writing about quilts, and procrastinating writing about quilts, and procrastinating learning how to make quilts, one thing I had done with great regularity was to talk to quilters. Not so much in the way I perhaps should have been talking to them—that is, formally interviewing them for this book. But whenever anyone would ask me, "What are you working on?" invariably I would shoot back, "A book about quilting."

At which point my inquisitor would usually blurt out one of two responses: either (a) that she (or sometimes he) was a quilter or that (b) she or he knew a quilter. So, much as one might learn more Spanish in a Mexican village than in a high school classroom, to my surprise I accidentally learned more about quilting than I realized just from chatting about it. (The lesson here being—and I hope this is true—that sometimes procrastination pays off.)

There were times, of course, when I did conduct formal interviews. I spent a day with Ricky Tims to research a piece I was writing for a magazine. And I interviewed Arlene Blackburn, she of the bizarre bleach-on-Elvis-quilt fate at the 2002 IQF. Arlene, as mostly all quilters can't help but do, told me about roughly eight thousand other quilters I would do well to talk to. Arlene is a quilter who enters her work in competition and who wins, and she knows other quilters who do the same. Arlene didn't just offer to put me in touch with some of these women; she went a step further and told me she would introduce me to them at IQF 2004.

Thus Arlene Blackburn became my fairy godmother at the festival. Among those she introduced me to were award-winning quilters Deborah Sylvester and Hollis Chatelain. Deborah didn't have a quilt in the 2004 show, but Hollis, as a matter of fact, did. And her quilt, Precious Water, won Best of Show.

This meant a couple of things. It meant a $10,000 purse for Hollis. And it meant front-page coverage in the Houston Chronicle. Now, you might think, with IQF being the biggest annual convention in Houston, that the winning quilt would always be a cover story. Not so. The reason Hollis' quilt merited such coverage in the eyes of the editors was because her technique was viewed by some of the more traditional quilters as "controversial."

Rather than piecing together her quilt top, Hollis paints on whole cloth, which she then layers with batting and a back. The effect is a quilted painting, or a painted quilt. While I never heard anyone out-and-out make disparaging remarks about the quilt, even among the group of women I attended the show with there was debate. Was this thing a quilt or wasn't it? (I said it was. Sarah disagreed.) While the reporter seemed somewhat even-handed in her reporting and quoted folks on both sides of the debate, the headline was, as headlines often are, a bit sensationalist: "Should Quilter Reap What She Didn't Sew?"

Being a punster, I appreciated the wordplay but not the sentiment. It was true that Hollis hadn't sewn multiple pieces together for the top piece, but certainly she had sewn. Her quilting, front and back, was astounding.

It was a busy weekend for Hollis, what with accepting the award, fielding reporter queries, dealing with the borderline cruel headline, and teaching classes. And you might think Hollis was left with a bad taste in her mouth for reporters. But Arlene put the good word in for me, and during a ten-minute break in one of her classes, Hollis agreed to sit down with me on the floor in the hall and tell me about her work.

Ten minutes is hardly enough time to interview anyone, even for a sound bite. Once Hollis dropped a few details about her life—her twenty years of humanitarian work in Africa, her photography work, her rather fast rise in the world of quilting—I knew a much longer talk was in order. Fortunately, Hollis—who does not have enough hours in the day to work on her quilts—set aside a big chunk of time for me.

Deborah Sylvester did the same. Being friends with Hollis and Arlene, Deborah peppered her tales with references to these two. By the time I finished talking to Hollis and Deborah, I almost felt like part of their circle. Here is what they had to say.

HOLLIS CHATELAIN

"What Dolly Parton says—bad press is better than no press—I think that that's really true. If it takes somebody saying something bad about you in order to get them to come out and see your work, they may come out and say, "Whoa—that's not at all what I thought," but they would never have come out to see it otherwise.

A lot of people are very comfortable with what they're doing. It's almost a risk to go into something new. And I think a lot of people don't like risk—they don't necessarily want it to go that way, because they're very comfortable with the way it is. Even though the quilt world is large enough and definitely open enough to have all different types of quilts, at the same time there are a lot of people that really like what they do, and maybe they don't want their boat rocked at all.

If you look back into the history, there have been quilters who have been doing stenciling on their quilts, and that in itself is a type of painting. They were doing that back in the 1800s. Of course it wasn't a majority of quilters, but at the same time it was still being done. Right now, the people who are painting quilts, they're not the majority of quilters, but it is being done. So it's not really that different. It's just that now our media loves to take things and make them a lot bigger than they are.

I won some large prizes in the past, but I'd never won Best of Show. When I won other prizes in the past, I don't think they were controversial, because two of the other large prizes were painted quilts also. Fabric has been enhanced with pigments, ink, paints, or dyes for many, many years. But maybe a lot of people didn't know that or understand that. When there was controversy about it, I wasn't surprised, because I have heard it in the past—that some people don't consider painted quilts to be in the tradition of quiltmaking. But at the same time, I've never had anybody come right up to me and say, "Your work does not deserve to be called a quilt," or anything like that. I think on the whole the quilting world is extremely positive—it's a wonderful place to be. People are very nice, very considerate, very kind to people.

Maybe this rocked their boat. I don't know. Maybe it was also that the journalist was just looking for something to make the front page. The fact that she did choose the most uneducated quilt person in the room [to ask his opinion] means that there are uneducated people going to quilt shows, and they're going to learn all that there is to see in the quilting world. The quilt world has changed considerably in the last thirty years. I'm not one of the people who paved the road for that. I'm lucky that I came in within the last ten years and was able to do the type of work that makes my heart beat faster; it makes me excited. I'm not really one who paved the road. There are a lot of other people who did it before me, and they made it easier for art quilters. And I'm just lucky to be able to come in and take advantage of that.

I do believe that the majority of the people in this world . . . first of all they don't realize how important the quilting world is in America, that there are twenty-two million quilters. I always call it the underground world of fishing—a lot of people fish, but they don't really talk about it much. So if you don't fish, you don't know how many people fish. Quilts—you don't know how many people actually quilt. Most people, if you mention the word "quilting," they think of a silver-haired woman sitting down at a frame with a bunch of other women and hand-piecing and hand-quilting everything. And it is all

Precious Water, by Hollis Chatelain. This quilt took Best of Show at the 2004 International Quilt Festival in Houston. Inspired by a dream the artist had, it is painted with six values of yellow and quilted with more than two hundred colors of thread. Photo courtesy of Hollis Chatelain.

Detail of *Precious Water*, by Hollis Chatelain. Photo courtesy of Hollis Chatelain.

Fatima's Son, by Hollis Chatelain. Photo courtesy of Hollis Chatelain.

Detail of Fatima's Son, by Hollis Chatelain. Photo courtesy of Hollis Chatelain.

traditional patterns, and it's usually in pastel colors and on and on and on. [But] it's not at all like that.

So if you bring an uneducated person into a quilt show, they're going to walk out with their eyes crossed, just because the variety and the technical part of it have gotten to such a level that it's just astounding. There are excellent, excellent technicians in the quilting world—some very smart people in the quilting world.

We make a very good living at it. My husband is my business manager. This is how we support ourselves totally. My quilt prices range usually three to forty thousand dollars, and they are going up. They're usually purchased by women or couples. There have been a few purchased by men. They're usually purchased by professional women. I'd say that 75 percent of my quilts are bought by quilters themselves. I sell a lot of my work on layaway.

My larger pieces we don't want to sell anymore. Because I put so much of myself into each and every piece. Even a small piece can take me a couple of months to make. Larger pieces take years to make, and many of them come from my dreams, so they really are very much a part of me. And my work sells very quickly. I'm in one of those wonderful, terrible positions where right now I don't have enough artwork. They say an artist without art is not an artist.

That's one of the reasons my prices are going up. Since each piece takes so long, basically what happens is my artwork sells in a shorter period of time than it takes to make another one. I have a list of people right now who will buy the work sight unseen—they'll see a photograph of it—who want to purchase my work, and they're just waiting for me to do it. It's just a question of time, because it takes so long. What happens is when your work disappears as soon as it's finished, you never have time to live with it, and it disappears into a private collection. The majority of my work is not being shown in public places, and then it's gone. And I am not very comfortable with borrowing my work back. I mean, I will ask for it back for a show, but I'm not very comfortable with that because I don't think it's very fair to the person who purchased it.

What we're attempting to do now is to hang onto some of the larger pieces like *Precious Water*, and we want to start renting my work out. I've heard of other people who do that. We would like to rent it out to organizations to bring attention to the issue of water. Because if it would disappear into a private collection or some public building, it would stay there and you wouldn't get to see it. If we can rent it, it can go to different places and bring attention to the problem of water that we have on this planet. That's really a goal that we have.

We worked for humanitarian organizations for many years in Africa. My husband worked with them for over twenty years. This is almost like coming full circle. Because if the artwork could bring attention to the issues that we actually worked with, then I think that that would be a contribution that we're very interested in making.

Her thoughts on winning awards and selling her work for great sums:

“ First of all, it's total disbelief, because I still can't believe people would pay so much money for my work. I always am surprised by it. When people actually say they want [my] work, I have a tendency to not necessarily react in the way you should when you sell a piece. I've actually said to people, "Are you sure? Do you know how much that costs?" I've done that several times and then want to kick myself because I can't believe I'm saying that. But it just is so surprising to me.

The first time that I won a big prize in Houston, it was very interesting because we had gone out and gotten home late one Saturday night. And I checked my e-mail, and somebody said, "You won Best of Show in a show in California." And so I wrote back to this person, and they were on the West Coast, and I said, "Are you sure?" And she wrote back and said, "I think so." And then she tried to find out and wasn't quite sure. I didn't find out [for sure] until Sunday that, yes, this was true—I won Best of Show.

So we went out, and plants are kind of our thing, and we bought some plants for the garden, celebrating. We came back and we opened a bottle of wine, and the whole family was there. And we were just laughing and having a good time, and the phone rang. I went and answered the phone, and it was Karey Bresenhan and she told me that I won one of the top six prizes in Houston. This is two things in one day, and it was really much more than I could handle. And I started to cry. And I couldn't stop crying, and I cried and cried. And she said, "But you're always in such control," and I said, "Well, you just don't know me."

My daughter—she must've been about eleven or twelve at the time—she looked up the staircase and saw me crying, and she ran and got her older brother. He came up and he didn't know why I was crying, but he knew I was crying and talking on the phone, so he's putting his arm around me, going, "It's okay. I don't know why [you're crying], but it'll be okay." And so I got off the telephone and went downstairs, and I just kept crying. I cried for forty-five minutes. I just could not believe that I actually won this prize.

And then I finally got it together and I thought, "I have to call my parents." I called my dad, and the moment I got on the phone, I couldn't even talk. I started crying again. And my father, who is this real "If you can't stomp on it, it doesn't exist" kind of guy, he just started saying, "It's okay. It's okay. We love you." That made me cry even more. I appear very differently than I am. I'm actually more of an emotional mess. [*She laughs.*]

I've had some requests for *Precious Water* for licensing type of things, and you know, you get into all these different types of things where you sign a contract to get into a show for one thing and somebody else wants to use one of your pieces for a brochure and you go, "How is that going to affect anything in the future?" So we really felt the need to contact a lawyer who dealt with this, because it's way out of our league. And one of the questions he asked me was, "How much money do you want to be making, and why do you want to be making money? Do you want to buy a new house or a new car, or what is your whole reason? Do you want five hundred thousand dollars a year?" I didn't know how to respond to any of that. I'd never even gone there. I was like, "Well, you know, I want to not be poor when I'm old, so maybe a little bit of retirement. And I like my house. We don't live in a big fancy house—that's okay. And I don't need to be driving a fancy car." But it's a whole different way of thinking.

Her thoughts about having lived in Africa and how she started quilting:

" It doesn't take very long to put things into perspective if you just stop and think about what the rest of the people in this world have, compared to Americans. The average American uses a hundred and fifty gallons of water per day. The average African uses four to five gallons every day. Whenever we would think about things being hard or not being able to purchase something that we needed or felt we needed, you just stop and think about how little the majority of the people in this world have, and they're much happier than

Americans. I think that that kind of put things back in place.

I really don't believe that money brings happiness. I think that it's rather what you do and the satisfaction. I like touching people—I don't mean making big changes in people's lives, but actually having that contact with people, whether it be through teaching or through my art or actually working with people in the third world. Because no matter where you are, people are people. They have the same emotions and feelings—they just have different outside circumstances. I think that's the thing that moves me the most. So if I'm in Hillsboro, North Carolina, in Russia or West Africa, you're going to find good people everywhere. It's up to you to figure out how to get along with those people. You can't go in and necessarily change them, but you can certainly learn from people all over the world.

I can remember living in Africa—and I'm not putting anybody down—but the people who had the diplomatic status and could go to the commissary and make great big salaries and put lots of money aside every month weren't any happier than me. [That status] doesn't protect you from getting certain illnesses and from being unhappy. When we lived in Africa, I'm not saying that we lived very poorly, but we were volunteers a lot of the time, and we definitely didn't have some of the benefits of some of the people in the highly paid corporations or organizations. But that wasn't why we were there.

I originally went with the Peace Corps, in 1980. I was a photographer. But they can't really use photographers in the Peace Corps, so I was what they would call a generalist. I think a lot of kids in their twenties want to change the world. I did. We all want to make it better. But as soon as you get there, you realize, "These people know a lot more than I do." I was an agricultural education volunteer, which meant that I worked with school gardens and animal husbandry—some very small projects. I didn't ever teach. I actually worked with them and gave advice. All pretty simple stuff, so I didn't need a whole lot of training.

I met my husband over there. He had been there for four years when I arrived. He rode his bicycle down from Switzerland. When he got to West Africa, he wanted to stop in a village for about a week, and actually four years later I arrived. He lived with a family for the first two years that he was there, and he worked in the fields and lived like that. He ended up going back to Switzerland to get funding, and he started some small projects. I arrived after he'd been there for four years, and it was love at first sight—it really was.

We were married traditionally in the village. We had our first child in a bush hospital, and she was delivered by African midwives by kerosene lamp. Then we left Africa, and we moved to Bedford, Pennsylvania, for two years, which was not like any America I ever imagined. It was in the Appalachian Mountains. It was really different. We thought we were going to be homesteading and all that. We were vegetarian and all-natural organic hippie-type people. We realized, "Well, this is very nice, but you can't make a living at it."

So we moved to Switzerland and lived there for two years, and I worked as a photographer at the University of Geneva and [as] a medical illustrator. My husband—we made a deal that we were going to have kids and one of us would always stay home with the kids. And he was waiting on a job and I found a job that first year, so I worked for a year. And then his job came through, and he was working with refugees, so we moved from Geneva up to the north of the country in a little teeny-tiny village of four hundred people. And I freelanced as a photographer and I worked in graphic design and stayed home with the kids. By then we had two kids.

We lived in Switzerland for two years, and we really wanted to go back to Africa. We found an ad in the paper [for] an ecology organization. So we ended up going back, and we lived in the capital. And I worked with solar cookers for three years, and my husband was the director of the organization. It was there that that I started actually getting involved with the textiles.

You could photograph, but you had to have a permit to photograph and you had to stand in line for a week to get a permit that lasted for a month. It was really just to discourage the majority of the people, and I very much understand why they did it. I think they did it to discourage the lack of respect. When people come in and visit third world countries, they feel they can barge right into anybody's compound or household and photograph anybody doing anything. There's a certain ownership Westerners feel when they go to countries where the level of poverty is very high. It's like they take away the dignity of the people.

It was very hot, so drawing was not very easy. My fingers kind of stuck to the pad. I started getting involved with the fabrics. I started collecting fabrics from the tailors, and little by little I taught myself to sew. So that's how I got involved in it.

When we lived in Bedford, I tried to make sheepskin clothing. I was really bad at it. So we had purchased a machine. I actually used to do these craft shows and sell it, but I shudder to think of it now. I don't know why anybody would've bought any of them. And we were so poor that we couldn't even buy whole sheepskin, so we used to buy the scraps from places that made sheep-skin clothing and I would make little moccasins and vests. So I guess something in me always wanted to put pieces of fabric together, but I am not a seamstress at all. The idea of me making clothing is very scary.

[Back in Africa, after Switzerland,] the wife of the director [of the program] got someone to donate a machine to me, and I started teaching women to quilt and make quilts. In the beginning I didn't have any batting, so I would go to the market and buy old blankets. I even have some of my first quilts—still have blankets in them.

I really thought a big needle means you have more dexterity, and so I had big stitches. Well, I didn't know anything about big or small. I was teaching myself. It wasn't very good. I had bought a book one year when we went to visit my husband's family in Switzerland. It wasn't a how-to book; it just had some quilting designs in it. And so I was trying to read that book at night and the next day teach these people what I had learned. Basically we all learned together. That was a lot of fun. I really enjoyed that.

I started teaching drawing, so I was doing a lot of things like that. Then we moved, and I started going to the factories and I started learning to dye my own fabric. I used to get the rejects from the factories, and they were just so pretty that I wanted to try and do it on my own, and so I started trying to teach myself to dye fabric.

I used to go to the ambassador's house with this other group of women once every week or once a month, and some people would crochet and some people would knit and I would do my little quilting stuff. I had a show of my work, and then two weeks later we moved and I started all over again, teaching drawing and color and art to children and doing my artwork and selling it.

That was actually when I wrote to Caryl Bryer Fallert and asked her if she'd teach me how to sew by correspondence. This American had photocopied the front cover of the *American Quilter* magazine, and it had a quilt on there that Caryl had made that I loved, and I said, "You know, I want to be able to do things like that." I never started out with "Go to your local quilt show and learn from the local teachers." The only thing that I had was photographs that people showed me that were in magazines. So I didn't know what the average person, the average quilter was doing. I thought, well, if she could do that, why couldn't I do that?

Well, Caryl didn't answer back, and that was in 1992. We happened to go back to the States for Christmas that year, and it was the first time in nine years we spent Christmas with the family, so it was a pretty big deal. While I was there, I found Caryl's number. I had sent the letter to the *American Quilter* magazine, written them a letter with an envelope in it with Caryl's name on it and asked them to send it to Caryl, and [I] sent it from Africa, so I didn't know if she had even gotten the letter.

So I called her and said, "You know, I am the one that wrote you from Africa." And there was this very long pause, and then she said—she's so nice—"Well, I'm sorry I didn't answer you, but I didn't know what to say. Teaching somebody to sew by correspondence is a little complicated." She was very kind and suggested I come back to the United States that summer and try to take a class from her. We just happened to be coming through the United States for home leave that summer, and so I was able to actually do that. And that's kind of how I got started.

On moving back to the United States and launching a full-time quilting career:

❝In August of 1996 we moved to North Carolina. And my husband was willing to give up his career for me to try to live my dreams of making a living doing this. I had a following in Africa and I was selling work, but definitely not what you could live on. I was also teaching. And when we came back to the States, I came back with forty pieces. Now, this is small and large, but I stopped selling my work for a period of time in order to come back with a body of work. We had some money set aside. My husband thought he'd do some consultation work. Caryl was a really big help in that whenever she would go and teach somewhere, she would give out information packets about me.

I hadn't lived in the States—we'd lived in Bedford, but I didn't consider that the States. We couldn't even have television there. In the wintertime we went for long periods without seeing anybody, because the winters were so harsh and we were so removed. So I hadn't really lived in what I had known as the States for sixteen years.

I left during the big hostage crisis and gas rationing and everybody was carpooling, and I came home to SUVs. And I came back with three kids who were almost fifteen, thirteen, and eight, and they'd never lived in the United States except as babies. They'd never gone to school in English, although I taught the older ones to read and write in English. All three spoke English and French—they were bilingual from birth. They'd always gone to French schools. Moving to a very small town in rural North Carolina was a major shock. It was probably the hardest thing we ever did as a family.

I missed Africa so much. I missed the spontaneity and the joy and the color and living outside so much. My husband had tried for years to get me to put my imagery in my work. I always drew people but never put them in my textiles. I don't think I had the confidence to do it. What happened was, after about six months I decided I was going to try to paint what I missed so much about Africa, and that was the people.

I had never painted before, but I tried to figure out how to use the dyes and paint them, so that way I could be with the people I missed so much. I had never been to a quilt show, so I didn't know what people were doing at quilt shows. I made a couple of pieces, and I made this great big piece and it had a baobab tree on it with a young girl and a woman. And I applied to the show in Houston with it [in 1997], and it won viewers' choice and it won a second prize.

[My quilt featuring the] busts of women's shoulders and heads, *Sahel*, was voted one of the top one hundred quilts of the twentieth century. That happened in 1999. It was another one of those things where somebody just wrote to me and said, "Did you know that Sahel was voted one of top one hundred?" And I said, "Oh, well, that's nice." I didn't know what that meant. I was so new in the quilting world and hadn't been to many shows.

Somebody else wrote me, and I thought, "I wonder what this means." And they gave me a list of [the other winners], and I looked at it and went, "Oh, these are some really well-known quilters. Wow." And so I called the *Quilters' Newsletter* and said, "A couple of people told me that *Sahel* was voted in, and what does this mean?" And they said, "You mean nobody sent you a letter?" and I said no, because I didn't even know if it was true. I didn't know anything about it. I guess I never had the real thrill of that, because I never understood what it was.

I'm very self-taught. Maybe that's one of the reasons people like me as a teacher. I think I give them the idea that they can do it too. I think that's really important. It's not about how much talent you have. There are millions of people that can draw very, very well, but they don't have the passion to do it. There are so many people who have the talent, but you have to have that something within you that makes you want to do it whether you're rich or poor or anything. It's all about the journey; it's not about the reward.

I feel so lucky because I get to do what I absolutely love to do every single day. I get up really excited to do it. That's why it was so frustrating to me when I pinched this nerve and I couldn't work. [Quilting is] my outlet in addition to being what I do professionally. I've been able to put those two things together. I think I'm probably one of the few people that is actually making a living doing this.

I think that a lot has to do with confidence. My parents just really, when I was growing up, they said that—they're very liberal—they felt you can do anything you want to do. I grew up with my mom making speeches for the ERA [Equal Rights Amendment] and marching in Washington. My parents said, "You can do anything you want to do. You just have to work at it enough." They've just always been like that. That's one of the reasons it was such a wonderful thing for me to be able to have them there in Houston and see that the freedom and the choice that they gave me allowed me to do something that I really love to do and to succeed. If you love it, it will come through. You have to be true. If you're true to yourself and true to the world, and you're not trying to hurt anybody and you're just doing good, it will open for you. The roads will open, and things will go.

On her Best of Show quilt, *Precious Water*, using dyes, how the process feels, and what she's working on now:

"I dreamed it in the spring of 2000. I worked for about a year and a half actively searching [for] imagery that I saw in the dream. Because the dream was very specific in that there were all the continents, and the people in it were definitely South American, North American, Australian, all of that, and then also they were using water how we use water. We use water to grow our food, we use water to wash with it, we drink it, and we share our planet with animals and they need water also. And so these things were very clear. And I really wanted to find imagery that when you looked at it you would say, "Oh,

Australia—kangaroo," or South America, Ecuador, with the hat and long braid, or an American farmer from North America. And I wanted a child in there. I really wanted to have Africa in there, but I couldn't get the imagery to work together.

For a year and a half I did drawings, and I searched for imagery. I even tried to photograph farmers. I photographed farmers all over, and I could never use any of the photographs that I had, because they just didn't fit with the rest. I could not draw a plaid shirt that looked real, and I really wanted the farmer to have a plaid shirt. I actually used [someone else's] photograph.

In that year and a half, I made the composition and got the drawings to size. From there I worked on it for six months, and then I pinched a nerve in my shoulder and I had to stop for six months, and then I went back again for six months. So it was a total of working twelve months to do just the painting and the quilting. And that's working full-time.

When I'm actually painting, I rarely am working on anything else until I get that painting finished, because my dyes will exhaust. Dyes are pretty picky. I just have to keep painting. It took me months to paint *Precious Water*.

I always seem to be on a deadline. A lot of times I'm forced into a time slot of getting one done. Right now I'm working on several different pieces at once. I'm drawing a piece with Jimmy Carter. I have a couple of other pieces drawn that I'm doing just threadwork—there's no painting in them. Then I have one piece that's painted, and I'm quilting it.

The dyes are like maple syrup [in consistency]; they're thicker than water. They're fiber-reactive dyes. They are permanent and colorfast, more colorfast than manufactured fabric. Dyes are not forgiving. You can't correct it. You cannot make a mistake. There are always mistakes in your drawing—I notice, but I hope other people don't notice if things are off a little bit. Sometimes you don't catch them till later, and then you just have to hope that other people don't see them.

The biggest quilting mistake I've made was hand-quilting a queen-size quilt with a fat batting in it, quilted every half inch. I bent and broke many needles.

My most satisfying quilting moment was selling a very bright wall hanging that I didn't really like, and other people were thrilled with it.

—*Sharon Weaver, Round Rock, Texas*

On the whole, there's not a whole lot you can do about it. I have had some problems and have had to go back and redo something with acrylic, very small areas. But when you paint with paints after using dyes, they sit on the fabric—they don't adhere to the fabric. [With] dyes, you can't go lighter—you can only go darker—and so if you paint something too dark and it's totally screwed up, that's a pretty major problem.

I didn't give a whole lot of information on *Precious Water*, because I did it in a way that I haven't seen anybody else do, and it's a technique. I don't think it's really hard to figure out, but some people cannot figure it out, and I think I'd rather keep it to myself.

When I did *Blue Men*, there was a certain serenity within me and a feeling: "Of course I can do this." There was no hesitation in it, which is quite unusual for me because I always enter a piece feeling like I am never going to be able to do this. Sometimes I look back at this work that I've just killed myself to do and I think, "Did I really do that? How did I do that?" When you see it a couple of years later, you go, "Oh, those mistakes haven't gone away."

A lot of times I think I've moved forward, and that's a very positive thing. I get this feeling that comes from a memory of it, of my struggles through it and how I felt about it, and what the piece means and why I chose this over that. It's very hard for me to look at my work with totally neutral eyes and see it as other people see it the first time that they've ever seen it, because it's so much a part of me. I think that even my family, they have a very hard time. Being in Houston and seeing their reaction to people's reaction to my work is something that I don't think that they can quite . . . can see how other people feel about it or see it, because they hear about it [from me and] they see me struggling.

When I actually get something right, it's like, "Come here! I did it! I got it right!" Right now I'm drawing Jimmy Carter, and I have to do these totally rendered drawings in color in order to have the finished piece look like him, because it's only going to be done in red—he's not going to be painted—and I've just never done this before. I will do a line drawing on the quilt, so there won't be any shading at all and it won't be in color. It will just be places of highlight and shading. It will look like one of those fill in the numbers pictures. I would like to go to him and show him this piece.

DEBORAH SYLVESTER

Deborah Sylvester, friend of Hollis and Arlene and an award-winning quilter herself, was, until her husband's recent retirement, a military wife. Which means she moved a lot. These days the family is in California, where Deborah is very content as a housewife and a quilter.

She started working at a Jo-Ann fabric store when she lived in Virginia Beach years ago. She recalls the day a woman came in, carrying a traditional quilting book. The woman was buying a ton of fabric—enough to make every quilt in the book—because she was going to move to Italy for three years. Inspired, Deborah decided she wanted to take up quilting. Then, like a lot of us, she procrastinated. But she never forgot the book.

Later, when she was working at a Wal-Mart, she saw a quilting magazine. Inspiration returned to her, and she says she made "the ugliest quilt." She was very proud of this ugly quilt (a story that resonated with me). And thus was born another stunning quilting career. Here's her story.

" Eight years ago, I'm pregnant with Kyle and watching that show *Simply Quilts*. And they had this lady on, and she was making the friendship star block, so I took notes, you know. It looked easy enough. I had lots of fabric, just scraps, and you could use small pieces. I cut out these little squares, just the right size and everything. And I went to stitch them together—I think each block had, like sixty-two pieces, little triangles. I machine-stitched them together. I was so proud of myself when I saw the first one. Then I made the second block, and it wasn't the same size.

There was this quilt shop in town, just down the street from me. So here I am—I've got this big tummy, and I've got this little two-year-old in my arms. I used to "run away from home"—go to the store and leave my husband with the kids. He always knew where I was. But this time . . . I took Kelly with me. The lady had her store set up really homey. She had bolts of fabric on the wall; that's how she had her store set up. The rooms that were supposed to be bedrooms had beds in them with quilts thrown over them. She told me to put the baby down on the bed. So I'm walking through, and she says, "What's the problem?" And I said, "Well, I made these two blocks, but one isn't the same as the other." And she said, "Don't you have a quarter-inch foot?" And I said, "What is that?" And that's how it started.

But I swear to God, for two years I was working the traditional way. I even went and bought that book that that lady [in Virginia Beach] had, and I got ambitious and said, "I'm going to make a whole bunch of quilts out of this book." I made one, and I was like, "Oh hell no, not me and this shit anymore." It had lots of appliqué. I made it and I put the book down. I never used the book again.

It was then I decided, starting to lean towards . . . I'm not a traditional person. I don't like the old-fashioned colors, you know? So then I got brave and started designing my own blocks, and then I just thought I wouldn't use traditional fabrics. That's when batiks first came in. I was buying them from the quilting catalogs. I just fell in love with them.

By then we had moved to Louisiana, and I joined a quilt guild. I was in a store, buying fabric, and this lady says to me, "Oh, what are you making with it?" I said I'm going to make a quilt. And she says, "Oh, you know we have a quilt guild here in Slidell." She was so friendly. She told me when the meetings were. I had never been to a guild meeting. It was a really new guild. I went, and they were all so sweet. As a military spouse, you move so much you learn how to make friends real quick, so you put yourself in a situation where you meet new people. So I went to the guild meeting. And they were all very nice, and it was a really small guild—twenty members.

One of the ladies I got to know—everybody started talking about Houston. I'm like, "Houston? What's so special about Houston?"

"Oh! You don't know?"

I still didn't know what they were talking about. By then my son was almost two, and he was still nursing. And I had planned—I told my husband about this trip everybody was taking to Houston to this big quilt show, and I'd never been to a quilt show in my life. He said, "Oh, that sounds like fun, but what about Kyle?" And I said, "Well, I'll have to wean him." But I couldn't get him off the breast. I said, "What am I going to do? I have my plane ticket."

My husband said, "Just leave. He'll eat. He'll get hungry enough."

And I did. I left my poor little baby with no breast. I called home and said, "How's he doing?" My husband said, "He's drinking a bottle. He knows when he's hungry." I was in agony, all leaky.

My friend said to me, "I want to take a class that doesn't involve a sewing machine." I'm like, "Doesn't involve a sewing machine? You're going to a quilt conference. How do you not expect to sew?" On PBS they had this show.

This lady was making really cute things, but it didn't involve sewing; it involved this sort of chopping up of fabric and stuff. It was the snippets lady. So we signed up for the class. I had no idea what I was going to do. Totally new to me, because I'd only done blocks.

We got to the convention center. About an hour before class the teacher walked past me and my friend, and I went, "Oh my God, she's stunning. You mean to tell me we're taking a class from Barbie?" It turned out she was very sweet, even though I was so exhausted I fell asleep during the slide presentation, which was the first half hour of the class. That was embarrassing.

The picture I took with me to remake [using fabric snippets], my husband picked it out. I couldn't decide what I wanted. I really liked this one my husband showed me. It was simple. By then I had learned to dye fabric. I'd been experimenting with a lot of stuff. By the end of that class, she said, "Oh, I like your quilt. When you're done, here's my card. Call me. I want it for my next book."

I thought, "You're so full of shit." She was serious. So I come home, and a friend of mine who is a local teacher, I was bugging her for all this advice. [When] she saw my thing, she said, "Why don't you remake that in a bigger size and you can enter it in a quilt show?" And I'm like, "Oh, please, give me a break!"

I entered my first competition in '99 and got in with two pieces at the Mid-Atlantic Quilt Festival in Williamsburg. One quilt had suffered so many tragedies. First of all, I was afraid to quilt it. I did the top, but Cindy Walters said [she would] quilt it. She was living in Seattle at the time. So I sent it off to Seattle for her to quilt it. We were on a deadline because I had to bring it back to photograph it to enter it in the show. That Christmas Day we had terrible snow in Seattle, and you couldn't travel for a few days. The airports were closed, and that means the mail stayed on the ground at the airport. The quilt had been quilted and sent back to me, but it got stuck in the mail, sitting at the Seattle airport for about a week.

By the time it got back to me, the box was all battered and wet. And I managed to finish the thing on time and photograph it and didn't think I would enter, because I remember saying to my friend Nancy, "Imagine going through all this, and they're just going to say, 'Thanks, but no thanks.'" And they sent me two letters saying, "Congratulations! You've been selected as a finalist." So this was . . . you're talking only two months after I learned the

A Moment in the Shadows, by Deborah Sylvester. Photo courtesy of Deborah Sylvester.

Lady in Red, by Deborah Sylvester. Photo courtesy of Deborah Sylvester.

technique. So then I had decided, "You know what? This doesn't involve a straight line or a triangle." And I stopped using blocks, because I had found what I could do.

All the technique was, was getting fusible web onto fabric and just cutting it up and making little pictures with it, very abstract-looking. Whereas I use it as paint. When I teach classes, I try to get people to understand that I think of my fabric as a paint palette so I can blend the fabric. I have to have a specific kind of fabric to start out with.

There are so many talented people, but it's who you meet—the universe puts these people in your path. Had I not gone to Houston, I would've never met any of these people, learned something new, and found I could do all these different things. The technique is basically a technique you can do anything with. If somebody teaches you how to paint, the person who taught you how to paint can't take credit for your talent; they just taught you how to paint. It's where you go with it. You can continue to paint boxes and trees and

Do You Dream in Color? by Deborah Sylvester. Photo courtesy of Deborah Sylvester.

flowers, or you can do something else, right? For us, I think, all I can say is, I do what I like to do.

I've taken two years off. I'm just coming off a self-imposed hiatus. I had a tummy tuck, and I had to take six months off for that. I wasn't . . . I'd had ten surgeries in the last maybe twelve, fifteen years, and I know what it's like—it's very stressful. I had been working so fast and so intensely, because when I'm working on a piece, it's all the time. I do it quickly, and then months go by and I do nothing. But when I start working, I'm always working. When I'm not working on the piece, I move it from the sewing room to whatever room I'm at. So if I'm in the kitchen, I make a place for it on the wall, hang it up so I'm always looking at it and thinking about it. That's the way I work.

But nobody can work like that all the time. So I take the time off. I had been doing it so much. I knew I was having this surgery and it would take six months to recover. And I knew realistically there was no way I'd have the energy to do it—I was having major abdominal surgery. And then the rest of the time—it was sort of devoted to getting my kid in kindergarten. And then my husband was retiring [from the military] and looking for a job. We didn't know where we were going to live. It was all about my family. And then he retired in June, and it was all about, "Wow. We have to live a regular life."

Two kids, new schools. My youngest, they diagnosed him with ADD, so he needs extra help, and my husband is never around because he works the swing shift. Before, when he worked the regular day shift, he did homework with the children. He doesn't do homework now. It's hard to get started [on quilting again].

Hollis has always been a great sounding board for me. Because of the way I work so intensely, when I'm done, it could be six months before I do anything, before I have an idea in my head. It used to bother me. I used to think I'd lost it completely. And I'd think, "Oh my God, I'm just a fluke. I have no talent."

I didn't want to be a one-hit wonder, like that band that sang "Afternoon Delight." Hollis would talk me through it. She was the one who started me on these exercises I would do every day, which is just putting pencil to paper. It doesn't have to make sense—just draw something and go on. She's been helping me. She actually . . . when I said I needed to take some time off, she's always said to me, "Okay, what's the big deal? You need to take this time off. You can't expect, with all the stuff going on in your life, to be able to create anything." She said, "Why don't you just go ahead and live your life?"

The ironic thing is, Hollis' piece that won this year, *Precious Water*, it was supposed to be finished last year. I remember she was rushing, trying to get it done. I remember I said to her, "I'm going to give you some advice you always gave me. You have to just take some time off. Have you got a piece off for this other show?" She said yeah. I said, "How 'bout taking some time off and relax." She said, "You know, you're right."

All of my best friends are what I call my quilting friends. I met them all through quilting. And we may not see each other all year, but we'll see each other at Houston and it will be like it hasn't been a year. The girl I room with every year? We met in a line in Houston going to that fashion show [part of the Quilt Festival]. That was in 1999. We've been friends ever since. And hell, she doesn't need to share with me; she can afford the room. I need the roommate.

I wasn't planning on going to Houston this year. I go every year, but I have to skim off the grocery money through the year to save up for it. Like I said, my husband was enlisted in the Marines; we didn't make any money. What happened was, I wasn't planning on going. I didn't have a dog in this hunt, meaning I didn't have a quilt in the show. I've had a quilt in the show every year I've entered since 1999, and I didn't enter this year. I sat it out

Hollis called me and said, "I just got a call from Karey." When they do the judging, they call you [before the show] if you're a winner, but they never tell you what you won. They'll call you if you're one of the top six. She said, "I got a call. I've got one of the top six prizes. And why aren't you going?" I said, "It's a little thing called money, and Lawrence doesn't have any time off because he's new in his job." She says, "You have to come. I want you to come."

So she's begging my husband on the phone to find some way to do this. He went to work and talked to his boss. He banked time, went into work two or three hours early. A girlfriend of mine down the street, her husband is a retired colonel. She said, "I would do anything for you. I'll pick the children up, and I'll come at five thirty in the morning." I said, "You're crazy. I wouldn't do that." Lawrence took the children to school and got to work late, and my friend kept the children [after school].

It was so nice of Hollis to insist that I come. I said, "I have no money." She said, "Don't worry about it." I got a plane ticket real cheap. I basically paid for three meals while I was there.

I went. She won Best of Show with that same quilt she'd been trying to finish for last year's show. She wasn't even planning it for this year. The judges aren't the same, so there's no telling if last year's judges would've chosen it. It's so unique.

Houston is a sort of weird environment where for fifty-thousand people you're a superstar. But it's sort of like living in a fishbowl. I've had a couple of experiences—I wouldn't say cattiness, but you have to understand, bottom line, this is a business, okay? A majority of people who go are going to a quilt show and they're there to enjoy and take classes. What you have to understand is there are people who latch onto you for many reasons, and a lot of them want to . . . I call it sucking out your energy.

I don't think I'm that unique, okay? But my work is very different. You don't find quilters who do the kinds of subjects I do, number one, and the human face is really difficult to do. When I moved here, there was nobody doing that. It was Hollis painting faces, and I was doing my thing and I was getting into the shows. I started teaching, but very limited because I can't leave my children and say, "I'm going away for three days." The money is fabulous, but I don't live near family and have the support network where I can leave my children.

In two of my last pieces . . . I started doing abstract work to keep myself from being bored stiff. And then I started putting the two of them together. I put figurative and abstract together, which apparently no one else was doing, and that works fine for me. My first attempt was by accident. I had drawn the abstract on transparency and the face on transparency, and they were just sitting one on top of the other on the table, and that's how it worked out.

It is basically fabric attached to fusible web. Only the faces are done in fusible. The bodies are done in fusible, and everything else is machine appliqué. I stitch into everything. I don't have to—I do it for texture. The fusible I use is one you don't have to sew around. It bonds with the fabric. It's called Steam-A-Seam Two. You don't have to stitch through it. I do. Because if not, it will just be like bubbles. I don't put a needle to it until I'm quilting it.

A lot of people feel fusible work isn't any good. Then there was this controversy about the life of fusible webs and [how they're] not going to last a lifetime. Okay, it's art. Nothing lasts forever. The way the testing was done, they tested it in the lab. It's the same thing they said when people started using monofilament thread—the invisible thread. The quilt police are always out there.

Remember that movie *Alien* where you got to see the queen alien give birth? There's one giant quilt police, and she constantly pumps out new ones, gives birth to them like a queen bee, and they come out knowing what to say: "Always use cotton thread, cotton fabric, cotton batting, cotton, cotton . . ." And they say stuff like, "A quarter-inch seam—you need a quarter-inch seam . . ." Whose rule is that?!

I took Ricky Tims' "Quilting Caveman Style," and I felt totally liberated. [In] this workshop I teach called "From Doodle to Textile Art," I tell them, "Nobody's going to judge you here. You can do whatever you want. This is your idea of your doodle."

And we're not doing little doodles. It's sweeping motions on the page, and you just go on. You free yourself. And a lot of these women can't do it. And so I say to them, "Okay, close your eyes. Before we start, breathe deeply. Put yourself in an open field. There is nobody around for miles. You're just by yourself. It can be field of flowers. It's of course a sunny warm day, not too hot, not too cold. It's not humid. It's just a beautiful day, and you can do whatever you want, and, oh yeah, you're naked. There is nobody to judge you."

One woman will say, "Can I have on my nightgown?"

I'll say, "I'm sure you've never seen yourself naked . . ."

I always start my classes like that, where you put yourself in that space where nobody is around, nobody's going to judge you, nobody's going to say that's bad. And they all feel so liberated when you tell them nobody cares. It doesn't matter if the seam is a quarter inch. We're going to cut it up and put it back together. It doesn't matter. There's no pattern for it. There's no rule. I think a lot of quilters, given the opportunity, would gravitate toward it.

There are a lot of people who just like structure. They like straight lines and points. I don't do straight lines and points because I can't—I know my limitations. I'm just telling the truth. I do what I do because I can and it looks good.

When I do my workshops, I know most people don't think they have an artistic bone in their body. In fact I got an e-mail from someone I taught last January. She said she was so inspired by my class. You get people—there's got to be one you inspire in the class. And it's just because you tell them there are no rules. I think more people would be attracted if they realized that what [their] idea of a quilt is, is not what's going on now.

I never say, "I'm a quilter," because then people instantly think of a grand-mother quilt on the bed made with old blouses or whatever. I always say, "I'm a textile artist," and they say, "What's that?" because they're not sure what that is.

I live across the street from my local quilt shop owner. I pop in and out of her house. We are complete opposites. She is a traditional quilter with the rules. We get along fine. She does fabulous work. In the summertime I'll see her out there, just working her ass off cutting with that rotary cutter, and I think, "You know, I'm so glad I don't do that." Because it's so precise that if you get it wrong, there is no real room for mistakes, right?

A *Moment of Peace* didn't start out like that. I had the imagery, the face, and I didn't know what I was going to do. I just started doodling on a piece of pa-per. I was just sitting there watching TV and started making these rectangles and making them look like little bricks and stuff. The face started in the cen-ter. And I had the little bricks behind and drew it out. I always draw my stuff out many times. My final drawing is the actual size. And then I have to make three copies off that. So I draw a lot.

I had it hanging on the wall for days. There was something about it that didn't look right to me. And my husband is looking at this thing staring at him every morning when he gets up, because it's hanging on the closet door. [He says,] "Are you ever going to start this?" I was like, "I don't know. There's some-thing wrong with it. I don't know what it is." He said, "It looks fine to me."

You know what it was? I cut it up and I moved things around. Those red strips? That's what made it for me. Here's another one of the secrets. You see what looks like little black lines, like shadows? That's a Rub-a-Dub marker. I drew on it! You tell me the rules. That's a laundry marker from Wal-Mart for two bucks! First I tried painting it, and the paint started to run, so I said that won't work. Then I tried Sharpie. Sharpie's not really permanent; it leaves a sort of yellowy color. I needed true black, so I researched it on the Net and I found out a Rub-a-Dub will give you true black and will not wash out or fade or change colors. It makes sense—it's a laundry marker. The quilt police would say I should've appliquéd it. Who's going to confront me? People talk behind your back.

I remember one time I was at a guild meeting. It was the last time I actu-ally brought anything to the guild for show-and-tell. I was president of the guild by then. I got up to show my piece—I would always go last because nobody would want to follow me. I would feel so bad. I'm like, "I just want to share my work with everybody else. I'm just a quilter at heart and want to show it to the guild." I hear little comments like, "God, do I have to go behind her? Nobody's going to look at my crap."

I got up one day—it was with my last piece I did—and what happened was, I stood up and I was about to take it up and I heard this woman go, "Oh God, not another one of these. Goddammit, can't she do anything else?" And that was the last time I got up for show-and-tell. I know [that woman] doesn't like contemporary work. There are a lot of people who don't think contemporary work should be called quilting. The definition of "quilt" is "three layers held together by thread."

The thing is, it's so weird. What is wrong? We're still quilting. It's just another way of constructing it. There are a lot of people [who think] if it didn't take you ten years out of your life and you didn't bleed all over the quilt, then it's not worthy.

I can't tell you the last time I made a quilt for my bed. When I want something for the bed, I go to Bed Bath and Beyond. My stuff is for the wall. I made one quilt for my bed—when I had a queen-size bed. Now I have a king-size bed. Do you think I made a quilt for this? Hell no! I made a king-size quilt once in my life. It was for a friend. I swore I would never do that again. No way. It was something simple, but it just took too much energy out of my life. It was too much to handle. It didn't inspire me. I felt like I was just laboring. That's why I don't do commission work.

Most quilters don't look at [quilting] as an art. The majority of quilters out there are like, "Well, it's a nice little craft. I make quilts for my grandchildren for the holidays." I wish a lot more people knew what was going on and had a different idea of what quilting was, you know. I don't know—it's kind of a shame to call it just "quilting" because [that term is] just so general. If people only realized that the art quilt was out there and how profound some of that work is and how long it's been going on. We're just sort of this unknown entity.

When you mention quilts, people thinks of blocks and that's it. Nobody ever thinks it could be anything else. I think Hollis' work is going really . . . it's made a big step for it to get on the cover of that newspaper, [for] all us little peons who are working nontraditionally, like Arlene and her felt work.

I was having a conversation with a friend of mine who lives in Oregon—

Sandy. She's a quilter too. She's won lots of prizes and stuff. We were joking around one day, talking about how people think of quilters as little old ladies in sensible shoes. One day I said, "If they only knew we were young and good-looking." And she said, "You know, some magazine should do a story about the younger quilters and the whole nontraditional quilters—the black ones, the Indian ones—and we could call it 'The Babes of Quilting' and do a glamour shot of us!"

One of my most satisfying quilting moments to date was making a cancer quilt for a friend, with blocks from her family, friends, and coworkers. Everyone wrote a story about their block. I combined the stories into a book with a picture of the quilt block on each story so my friend would have everyone's personal thoughts with her always.

When we presented her with the quilt, she had no idea, as she thought we were going to the restaurant to celebrate a friend's birthday. She was just amazed. Her daughter had come in from Nebraska, and a lot of her friends were there. We had the quilt displayed, and several of us took turns reading about each block in the quilt.

Another time, a quilt sister in the SLUTS [Sophisticated Ladies United to Sew] quilt group I belong to was getting married. It was decided we needed to make her a quilt. I copied paper-pieced patterns from Carol Doak's book and handed them out, along with the background fabric, to our group to make stars.

Karen, the girl we were making the quilt for, saw us and asked what we were doing. Being quick on my feet (a good liar), I told her I had gotten myself into a bind and had promised the girl I worked with (Jeannie) a quilt, and several people were helping me out with blocks. However, I told her [that] since she was getting married, she wouldn't have time.

Thinking we would put the quilt together at retreat, I was surprised when Karen said she was coming to retreat. So I took the box labeled "Jeannie's Star Quilt" to retreat, and we all worked on the top with Karen there. She never caught on. At the next guild meeting when it was time for show-and-tell, Karen helped me hold the quilt. I ask her to read the label, and that's when she realized the quilt was for her! It was awesome how we pulled off the big surprise. —Melissa Picha, Fort Worth, Texas

1 2

You Can't Break Rules
You Don't Know

Way back at my first quilt show, IQF 2003, I remember being pulled to ward a quilt that made me catch my breath. It was a picture quilt, and the image was of geese. Now, I can take or leave geese as subject. But what grabbed and held my attention was the way the work was done. Photographic in reproduction, presented on a stark, dark, solid background, this work had a crispness that appealed to me. Moving closer and educating myself with the accompanying written description, I discovered this was a painted quilt.

Walking through the show, I came across a few more quilts done in the same way, and each was done by Inge Mardal either alone or in collaboration with Steen Hougs. Talking with Sarah about their work later, I found she was less impressed with this painting technique. She wondered if maybe I was drawn to the work because it was accessible.

There's no denying Inge and Steen's work is very accessible. But I've been checking it out now for a number of years, and I still get the same feeling every time I view their work. I fall in love with it. Because they manage to convey something—the spirit of the creatures they capture—with each quilt.

At IQF 2004, I was happy to see that, among a good number of quilts that Inge and Steen had hanging, they received a $5,000 award for innovative artistry for a quilt called Poised, which featured a squirrel. In my mind, Inge and Steen, whom I'd never met, were rock gods of quilting, consistently turning out hit after hit. I longed to meet them but figured I'd attempt a phone interview sometime after the show.

At some point, though, I wished out loud that they would materialize. A bystander said, "Oh, they're up on one of the balconies, having lunch." And so, using only the small photo that accompanied their award-winning quilt as my guide, I made a mad dash up the endless escalator, breathless in my pursuit, feeling eager and shy, hoping to meet them with the sort of burning desire I once reserved for lead singers.

I checked one balcony and then another. Once, I spotted a woman alone, wearing black, her gray-streaked hair pulled up. She had a European look about her, but I told myself that her solo status excluded her from being Inge. Still eager, but now with that little voice in my head telling me there was no way to find these people in such a crowded scene, I began an aimless wander, my feet moving slowly in the direction of the escalator.

Which is when I spotted a man, also in black, moving with a confident stride in the direction from which I'd just come. I burst upon him. "Are you Steen?!!" I shouted.

He was Steen. And he took me to Inge, who was the woman I'd earlier decided was not Inge. I didn't give them much time to speak, gushing over their work, speculating that they must be very tired (though Steen insisted they were not), and begging them for an interview. Really, there was no need for begging. Steen handed me his business card and suggested I e-mail him my questions so that he and Inge could have time to mull them over.

Later, I ran into him again as he took a turn standing in front of the squirrel quilt, fielding the questions and unrelenting praise from onlookers. Inge appeared briefly—obviously she prefers to let Steen be the public face of their work. Again I smiled at her, again overeager but not ashamed of my obvious and unbridled joy. I don't suppose if anyone had told me when I was sixteen and dreaming of marrying Bruce Springsteen that one day I would feel my heart beat faster upon meeting quilters whose work I not only admired, but through whose work I was able to first feel passion for the art of quilting.

I sent Inge and Steen a list of questions then, and here is how they replied via e-mail:

Q. The first time I attended a quilt show, I was immediately drawn to your work. It leapt out at me and it moved me. Whereas I find your work delightful and accessible, I think some viewers have some difficulty because the pieces are painted, not pieced. I know this year's winner, Hollis, faced some controversy because she also paints her quilts. How do you feel about this controversy?

“ This controversy should be taken with a grain of salt and reference should be made to the period where machine quilting was introduced. Machine and hand quilting now coexist happily in a broader context than was the case before.

Consider Inge's situation: she started quilting in 1995 with purchased fabrics only and following traditional techniques, although she always added a touch of her own, which brought it further out on the axis of expression—to the point where fabrics alone were not enough.

A move to Brussels in 2000 with the entire stash in store for 7 months gave the incentive to take full control of the process. Gradually and very discretely we started to apply paint, so in this way *Crows' Nest I* and *Crows' Nest II* could be considered as the initial steps towards our present painting techniques. Also, at the moment, as a consequence of sparingly applied paint and a larger role for the graphical aspects of the design, Inge's quilting techniques developed significantly and took new directions.

We continued this initiative because we felt that the combination of painting and quilting was well suited for implementing the motifs we increasingly chose from nature, and for rendering features and emphasizing aspects we wanted to emerge from the quilt. The technique also gives us a wider scope for expressing our personal emotions and feelings in a quilt (as opposed to a possibly pretty, but unemotional, "photographic" reproduction of a scene).

So, the fact that we paint should be seen as our present way of working

Poised, by Inge Mardal and Steen Hougs. Winner of the Maywood Studio
Master Award for Innovative Artistry at the 2004 IQA Judged Show. Photo by Jim Lincoln.

River of Life, by Inge Mardal and Steen Hougs. Winner of the Fairfield Master
Award for Contemporary Artistry at the 2005 IQA Judged Show. Photo by Jim Lincoln.

Pit Stop, by Inge Mardal and Steen Hougs. First place for two-person quilt, 2004 IQA Judged Show. Photo by Jim Lincoln.

Ringed, by Inge Mardal and Steen Hougs. First place for two-person quilt, 2005 IQA Judged Show. Photo by Jim Lincoln.

and not in any way as a way of differentiating ourselves from the mainstream quilters. As you can see, painting has gradually come into play in our studio and for the time being this is how we work—it's as simple as that.

The controversy to which you refer serves no purpose at all. Individually Inge and Hollis have chosen other directions for their creative endeavours, which, in essence, were determined by their striving to achieve desired effects between design, fabric, hues, values, and quilting.

From the point of view of awards in the various exhibitions in Quilt Festival, one should keep in mind that there are de facto more possibilities for traditionally made quilts to win prime awards than is the case for contemporary quilts. So, let's leave it up to the more traditionally oriented quilters, who have a problem with painted whole-cloth quilts, to take on the challenge and go for all the awards for which they are eligible.

Enough said on that—maybe the reporter behind the event this year in Houston is the only one who can use this controversy at all—and only if she/he had a bet with a colleague that she/he could get a quilt-related article above the fold on the front page of the *Houston Chronicle*.

Q. I interviewed Hollis and she told me she paints her quilts horizontally. You mentioned that your quilts are painted vertically. How challenging is this?

❝ Oh, it is challenging as well. Both methods have to be applied with great care to prevent bleeding, and for vertically mounted fabric the force of gravity also needs to be taken into account. However, this disadvantage is somewhat counterbalanced by the fact that the vertical approach allows us to step back at any time to evaluate the progress at a distance. In the answer below to your question on how we cooperate on a project, you will see that there is yet another advantage to painting vertically.

Q. What is the breakdown of responsibility when the two of you are working on a project? Please elaborate who plays what role from beginning until end.

❝ When we jointly work at a project (remember that Steen has his full-time job), issues like the selection of photos, simplification and fine-tuning of the composition (often by means of sketches), determining a suitable palette, and the process of applying the paint are all shared tasks.

When Steen has sufficient time available he may then give it a bash on the "canvas," allowing Inge to sew on another quilt in parallel. The way our studio is laid out allows her to follow the evolution on the "canvas" and in real time recommend corrective actions if it turns out too bright or too dark, is lacking contrast, etc. So, although there may be cases where Steen paints the most of the quilt foundation, the process is strongly influenced by Inge's suggestions.

It may sound as if Steen is remote-controlled from behind Inge's sewing machine. Be assured, it is not the case. We are far too different individuals to make this possible at all.

The concept phase, as we call it, typically goes like this: We seek inspiration in nature during vacations and, in particular, in bird-watching, which we find interesting and challenging (finding the sites, approaching the birds,

---

I always incorporate my late grandmother's clothes in all my quilts. My grandmother had five names. Her father's favorite, born the fifth girl of seven children, she was named Cleadith Marie at birth. Her father wanted a boy, and he called her Robert at home. From the time she was a baby, he took her riding on the tractor and taught her to ride, hunt, plow, and shoot on their cotton farm west of Fort Worth.

As soon as she started school, the family realized that she couldn't continue to be called Robert. So at home and school she then went by the name Bobbie. When her first grandchild was born—that's me—she taught me to call her "Nannie." Our family called her "Nannie" for many years. Over the years, Nannie and her husband, Poppy, became known as Nan and Pop. Upon her death, she was known to everyone as Nan. Cleadith Marie, Robert, Bobbie, Nannie, Nan. She was a special inspiration to me and taught me how to sew. I took up quilting late in her life.

I made a wedding quilt for my brother and new sister-in-law for their queen-size bed. I created a wave, a surfer's curl with a sunset in the upper right corner. Although I used all squares, I made the wave into a curve, including the white foam edges and deep blue of the undersea. The sun was pieced with raw silk rays that shimmered in the light. Most of the quilt was made from my grandmother's clothes. —Dana DeBeauvoir, Austin, Texas

---

etc.) to photograph. Now, birds are not always cooperative, so while we are waiting for them to be so, we look around for insects, butterflies and plants. This is indeed fascinating—and even more down at macro level.

In the evening at the hotel (over a glass of wine and/or at dinner) we discuss the day's harvest and already at this point ideas are formed for one or several motifs, moods and/or light-conditions that can be used as the basis for, or component in, a new quilt.

Homing in on the motif in this way subsequently allows us to return to the motif to further research the next day, and be more focused in order to improve our comprehension of light and shadows, hues and values that we had captured the day before. We try to iterate as much with nature as we can, while being out there.

Back home in the studio we try to recollect the impressions and pre-selections already made and narrow down the choices to a single photograph, or a group of photographs, on which we finally will base our design. The design process is normally supported by a series of sketches (before the era of digital photography, it was the other way around) for the purpose of simplifying lines and eliminating details—in other words to get rid of clutter and firm up the composition, as we want it and how we believe it will best support the motif and what we personally want to express in that new quilt.

We then discuss the palette and guidelines for values in the motif. At this point, when Steen is cooperating, Inge returns to the sewing machine while he mixes a series of, for example, muddled greens for a background, which we have decided shall be dark, but not black. The samples are discussed, one is settled for and Inge goes back to the sewing machine while Steen mixes a pot of paint and starts painting that background. In case there is a break and it takes too long (relative to a deadline) before he can complete the job, Inge grabs the brush and continues.

Once we are satisfied with the painted motif, the paint is sealed and the quilting process commences. At this point in time Inge will typically present a range of ideas for quilting she has developed during the painting process and together we decide which one is the most suitable, as well as the threads to apply.

Once quilted, it is squared and the binding (painted in matching/supporting colours) is applied and the quilt is headed for the washing machine. Thereafter it is hung vertically to dry before the photo session with our professional photographer.

Q. You mentioned that Inge works 8 hours a day, 7 days a week, when working on a project. How long might this process take? What's life like at this point? And when a project is finished do you have a ritual, perhaps a weekend trip or some other way to get reacquainted?

❝ Yes, we are so used to this schedule that it not perceived as a problem per se. There are times where deadlines approach faster than foreseen due to distracting non-quilting activities. In most of these cases Steen probably is the culprit. Inge has "le rigueur," as the French say. Without this rigour we would finish fewer projects per year and implicitly lose opportunities to also experiment with new ways of expression, compositions, quilting patterns, etc.

Such experimentation often takes us beyond the point of full control and provides merciless feed-backs on visions and ideas we had and felt should be tried out. Here the proposals by our son, Roland, for names in the category "Disaster 1," "Disaster 2" and so forth are absolutely to the point.

Q. I really got a laugh out of the titles your son gives to your works (Disaster 1, etc). How old is he? Is he an artist? Does he show any interest in quilting?

❝ Roland is 27 now and holds a PhD in computer science—so he cannot qualify as an artist in the context of your question. He has, however, since the childhood years had a flair for quickly rendering an expression, emotion, impression or scene by means of a pencil or paint and brush.

He has not been actively painting or drawing after the childhood years, but has nevertheless developed a razor-sharp ability to take in a piece of art, evaluate it and formulate his opinion on it.

Roland studied in England and stayed there after the university years and has a very busy professional and social life. It does not impede him, though, in pursuing musical skills and his broad interest in music. It appears, however, that he has a genuine interest in what we're producing, although he nowadays can only sporadically follow what's going on in the parents' studio in Chantilly.

Q. Because you are not from a place where quilting is prominent, perhaps you are not exposed to the stereotypes of quilting. For example, if you tell a non-quilter in America you are going to see some quilts, that person might get a visual image of a bunch of old women sitting around in church working on a quilt. Do you suppose the art has been different for you since you were not predisposed to such stereotypes?

"Although we are not from a region where quilting is/was prominent, our impression is that the notion of a quilt usually was linked to the image of a bed-spread made up of nine-patch or similar traditional patterns. But it was far from every home, which had a quilted bedspread.

When we were kids in Denmark no one would associate a patchwork with a "bunch of women," as you quoted it in your question, around a quilting project in church—not to mention a piece of art. Women just didn't gather in church to do such things—or anywhere else, for that sake.

Whether our approach to rendering motifs and creating quilts would have been different had we grown up in Santa Barbara or New York City, just to take some examples, is indeed difficult to say. Contributing to our individual style may be the fact that Inge has never taken a class (quilting or related) and Steen has never been subject to formal art education. We are self-taught.

Q. Along the same lines talking about stereotypes, how does it feel for Steen to be in a support role? From our brief interview it sounds as if you collaborate very 50-50 up until it's time to sew. Is that correct? Once the sewing begins, does Steen ever feel as if he is moving into a role (supporter) more traditionally associated with women? If so, is it difficult?

"Yes, as mentioned above, we do cooperate actively until the point in the process where quilting starts. As also said, Steen cannot sew, but how well the chosen quilting methods, styles, and colour scheme actually do match, are all aspects discussed in the studio, as they get applied in the process.

It is not—psychologically perceived by him—difficult to have the specific responsibility for the catering side of the studio sustenance.

Q. What has been a highlight moment of your lives together as quilters?

"When Inge kissed Steen at a given occasion related to quilting, which none of us remembers anymore—but he remembers the kiss.

Maybe it would be appropriate here to mention that we have been very pleased indeed to see our projects fare well in prestigious exhibitions around the globe. After a period with a relatively high level of success (measured by placements in such exhibitions), inevitably questions arise about the sustaining power of the artists in such a competitive field.

A highlight could in this context be considered as being the moment where we could take stock of the situation and name repeated representations of our work in the most prestigious and coveted (and imperatively also most competitive) exhibitions and shows at international level.

The absolute highlights are for us, however, linked to being searching for motifs and inspiration on a lovely coastline with dramatic seascapes, changes of the tide, birds around, smells of wild herbs, bushes, and flowers—and this wide horizon, which Inge in particular loves, and finds as important as vitamins.

Q. Have you had any major quilting disasters?

" Of course we have had crises in the production in the studio, which were conceived as "Disaster X, Disaster Y . . ." As mentioned above, such disasters do in particular appear when experimenting.

The really big disasters, as we see it, are the projects where we applied techniques with which we felt comfortable and well versed in—and where such projects just didn't work at all.

Q. What is the most difficult part?

" To keep Steen away from the kitchen and make sure that he pulls his weight in joint projects.

That was a joke, naturally (almost a joke . . .)! There are many time-consuming traps on the way from square one till a quilt is considered finished. As mentioned above, trying new concepts, for example, and making them work as intended, is not an easy task.

Q. Do you sell your quilts? If so, do you miss them?

" Occasionally we do sell a quilt and we have no remorse once it has parted. At the date of sale we have already moved further ahead on our evolutionary path to some new point, which no one knew when the sold quilt was originally created.

When working on a project, we are so concentrated and have our minds so focused on making the creative process on that particular quilt work our way that there is not much time available to send thoughts back in time to a quilt made in the past.

We could mention, though, that when a quilt returns after a couple of years of exhibition touring, then we are surprised over how much we have developed since the days when that particular quilt was created.

Q. I would say it seems you have had a spectacular amount of success in a very short period of time. Do you feel like there is any professional jealousy, where other quilters resent your success?

" No, we do not seem to have experienced direct expressions of jealousy.

We do, however, ask ourselves if jealousy actually does exist in the quilting world. As a matter of fact, we have always been approached with friendliness by other quilters and professionals in the quilting market. This includes the exquisite quilters with whom we compete and/or co-exhibit.

It's very relaxing to quilt by hand, and very creative to chose the pattern and fabrics. Buying fabric is addictive, and it's so much fun. When I start a quilt, I have a general idea and plan I start with. But the quilt usually "tells" me what it needs as I go along, so my finished quilts usually look somewhat different from the original idea.

A casual friend was very insistent I make a quilt with a University of Oklahoma and sports theme for her new grandson. I was really hesitant, as I knew nothing about OU—not even their team colors. I did a little research on the Internet, and I drafted a central block to piece, based on the OU logo of the interlocking O and U.

I happened upon some fabrics which also inspired me, so I decided it would be feasible. Next, I came across a quilt block setting called Road to Oklahoma, and another block which reminded me of a wheel—as in the Sooner Schooner.

I went from being completely annoyed that she would insist I do this quilt for her when I didn't want to, to being very excited about the possibilities and very happy with the results. —Loren C. Rice, Austin, Texas

We would like here to mention that having a quilt accepted in these coveted international exhibitions is a success in its own right. We have always regarded the acceptance of our proposals as a success.

Q. Do you have a favorite quilt?

"Amongst the quilts produced in our studio some remain longer in memory or, put differently, pop up more often than other quilts do due to the fact that they are more frequently used as references in discussions.

Some quilts we are very satisfied with from a design point of view, others from the points of view of the applied colour scheme and/or quilting methods.

Instead of pointing at a single favourite quilt (which would be like having to chose a favourite amongst your kids) we would rather approach this question by saying that the sequence of our quilt production can be regarded as kind of a diary illustrating our lives in various ways (e.g., vacations, moods, living, and working circumstances . . .).

So, have some days been "better" than others? No, they all build upon the previous days, somewhat like when a house is being built stone upon stone, and each day has contributed in its own way. It has in other contexts been said that hurdles overcome make you stronger. The diary, or our series of quilts produced so far, will inevitably reflect hurdles we have struggled with and eventually overcome. This, in a way, contributes to the fact that quilts can be very intense, maybe not only to us, but also to beholders at the various exhibitions.

And what about the days to come? We neither have medium- nor long-term plans for future quilts to be produced in our studio. Actually, we cannot even talk about near-term plans. Our production is more according to the proverb "Carpe diem" where intuition, moods, inspiration, etc. together make us choose the way of implementing the next quilt.

Q. What do you do when you aren't quilting?

"Ohhhh!

Well, going hunting for inspiration in nature with our cameras, sketchbooks, drawing paper, and crayons and pencils etc. during vacation periods is one extra-quilting activity, which we indeed enjoy. Since we have no servants or errand boys we do have to keep the apartment clean ourselves, do shopping, wash the linen, and all those mundane no-fun activities.

Q. Does Inge have a favourite sustenance food to keep her going when she's sewing?

" Inge loves first-quality cheese, which we buy in our organic food store. Usually they are of French origin, but Swiss and Spanish mountain cheeses also find their ways to the cheese tray.

[She also enjoys yogurt.] Otherwise she relies on the output from Steen's cuisine. Junk food is out of the question.

Q. Is Inge's aunt who helped with her knitting still alive? If so, what does she make of your success?

" No, unfortunately Aunt Anna passed away a year ago. She probably died intellectually some years earlier due to Alzheimer's but, relating her death to quilting, we could mention that she died on the day of the Silver Star Salute dinner at Quilt Festival 2003.

Aunt Anna surely would have been very happy to see Inge sustain her interests in working with textiles. She also would have had a genuine understanding for the fact that there is no time for knitting anymore.

Q. What else would you like to tell me about your lives as quilters?

" Outside a quilt show it is difficult to point at someone passing by and say that he or she probably is a quilter. There is no set norm for hairstyles, fashion, etc. in quilting circles.

What one cannot see on the outside is that quilters appear to be people with a wide range of interests in related aspects: from textures to haute couture demonstrated at the cat-walk. Colours and changing shades and values are also of more interest to the observant quilter than to others.

To be a quilter also involves dealing with three dimensions, since the quilting process so significantly augments a motif. This is reflected in the continued interest at quilt shows to have the rear side of a quilt turned so that it can be inspected and pass on a deeper knowledge about the quilt. Here lies the root of the "white glove" ladies.

The rear side of a quilt reveals the effort and care put into a given project. An experienced quilter will immediately have an appreciation for that aspect, we would think. This may be the reason why we get surprised when approached with the question: "How long did it take you?"

As Inge puts it, what meaning does it have whether it took 2 weeks or 2 months to complete a given quilt? The final result, the quilt in front of the beholder, should be viewed as a piece in its own right, and not according to statistics on yards of thread, stitching density, etc.

The following anecdote kind of illustrates this: A collector asked a famous Japanese painter to make him a piece of art. OK, said the artist. Next year the collector asked about the progress. I'm still thinking, was the answer. This went on for 10 years, until the artist finally invited the collector to come with him to his studio. There he took out a canvas and in 15 minutes he produced an excellent piece of work. The collector says with great frustration that he had waited 10 years and it only took 15 minutes to make—and he understood nothing anymore. The artist calmly explained. No, it took 10 years and 15 minutes!

OK, we cannot produce a quilt in 15 minutes, but we think that you got the gist of it.

I was making my granddaughter a quilt . . . just started making squares and decided to make it big enough for her youth bed. Not being a whiz at math, I asked my son, the college student, to figure out how many squares I needed. He came up with something like 960. Well, I eventually started putting them together and had enough for the quilt, pillow sham, and two or three baby quilts . . . So much for that college degree.   —*Sandra McCallum*

13

Peacing It Together

Jote Khalsa lives in a little town in Texas called Blanco. This town, known for its bowling alley and pie, is just down the road from another little town called Dripping Springs, known to the locals as Drippin'. In this same vicinity is Wimberley, where years ago Jote's mother, G.B., a midwife, opened a little store, Peacemakers, with some friends who wanted a community space where women could come and work on crafts and just be together.

Over the years, for a number of reasons, the shop changed—some of the original partners left, all of the crafts fell away except quilting, and the location moved from Wimberley to Drippin', where, eventually, Jote took it over. She likes to joke that, as proprietor of a quilting shop, she is "an enabler," but she's quick to add, with a laugh, "You gotta give me money to do it."

Someone stumbling upon Jote's little shop out in the country might just assume she's a small-town girl who never got out. They would be very wrong. Jote is small-town in that she knows most of her customers by name and can tell you a lot about their lives too. But this sense of community was actually born of a number of factors, none of them concerning small towns.

Likewise, Jote's shop is not just a retail outlet for fabric. She carries on the original vision of the store's founders, making her space welcome to all. From the pink mailbox out front (more than whimsical, it's a good, easy-to-spot landmark) to the kids' toys inside, Jote provides a sense of irresistible hominess. She doles out fat quarters, but she doles out a whole lot more too. I sat down one afternoon and asked Jote to tell me how she wound up in Drippin'.

" My mom opened the shop with another midwife, a retired midwife and another woman who was part of their mothers' group. Everyone took a project. It was quilting, knitting, basket weaving, cross-stitch. Each place was the size of a closet. The name "Peacemakers" came from picturing a bunch of women sitting around a table working on whatever they do with their hands, but a place where you could come together and talk and make peace.

Bit by bit, everyone's lives took pretty significant changes, and so, bit by bit, each one of them had to drop out. I wasn't involved; I was still in North Carolina. Then we moved back to Texas. Then I got pregnant, and that's when I started quilting.

My mom has always been like, "Oh, you're bored? Here . . ." She'd put something in my hand like, "Don't whine—make something" kind of thing. And so I grew up knitting, crocheting, weaving. When I was pregnant, my knitting was getting tighter and tighter and it just was not that enjoyable. It wasn't relaxing.

So Mama's like, "You know we've got the quilt store. I want you to make a quilt for your baby." I just went, "Okay. It's just another thing that Mama says, 'You've got angst? Make something!'" And so I started quilting and never turned back.

When Liam was about six months old, I needed a place to work and I started working part-time at the store, and bit by bit it kind of became my baby. At that point I lived in Austin, and I drove from Austin to Wimberley.

My mom and dad lived in Austin ever since I was two. They moved a house out here [to Drippin'] from Austin. My dad, he was bedridden—he had a brain tumor. There was a push to get out of town and into a peaceful environment. It made more sense to move the shop to Drippin' because it was closer to them.

My parents are Sikhs, which is a religion from northern India. Sikhism is not very old as far as religions go. What it came from is—my understanding of it—when the Hindus and Muslims were persecuting each other, burning people, disemboweling, this guy came forward and said [that] to kill in the name of God is wrong . . . So he left, and all these people gravitated toward him, and that's how it started. You can't kill people in the name of God. It's not one religion—parts of Hindu, parts of Muslim, parts of Sufi. People will say, "Oh, Sikh. That's a militant thing." There is a sect of Sikhism that's very militant, [but that's] not the one I grew up in.

My parents found each other in an ashram in Tucson because they started taking yoga classes. They moved in and lived in this communal-living ashram. And then they got sent to an ashram in Kansas City, and that's where my brother was born. And then they got asked to go start an ashram in Austin. We were in Austin from then on.

When I was in eighth grade, I went to India. I was such a very sharp but naive child, like sharp academically and totally naive socially. I can't believe some of the things I didn't see. I grew up in a very humble, very simple, very nonmaterial-based home. I was getting chewed up and spit out because I was letting myself be. Because I was in eighth grade. You always think you're different, and nobody gets you in eighth grade.

I knew that I was probably going to go at some point to India, but [the opportunity came at] the pinnacle of [my] being tortured for ridiculous social reasons and ridiculous material-possessions reasons like [the other students] just can't believe I can't have a pair of Guess jeans. It was the perfect opportunity. A friend of my family had applied for a scholarship for me, and I had gotten it. And so in the middle of eighth grade, that's when I went.

I went to boarding school. I went for two years by myself, and in the third year my brother came. There's a large Sikh community in New Mexico. They have a camp every year that lasts all summer long. I went all the time. So I was going to an unfamiliar country, but I wasn't at all going into an unfamiliar situation.

I went to two schools. The first school, the boys and girls were separated. There were probably eighty American girls out of six hundred students. A lot of the staff left and went and started another school. They joined the boys' and girls' schools and started a school down the mountain. It seemed like two hundred American kids out of four hundred total kids. There were plenty of kids from Afghanistan, Somalia, Malaysia—it wasn't just Indian kids. In most cases it was people who had wealthy parents whose parents were getting them out of bad situations, especially countries where you had to go fight.

I was so naive. We would come back once a year. I always felt like I had culture shock coming here [to America]. I never had culture shock going there. I felt very, very at home [there].

I look back on it as an adult with my own children and wonder why I wasn't bothered more. Here when somebody's standing on the corner [begging], you watch everyone in their car, myself included. You watch people pretend they don't know that person there. There's so much poverty in India [that] if you're there, you're in it. I always think I could've been more of a social activist. When you're in your high school years, that's when you do that. Not that you can't do it now, but I was there, I had the attitude—Up with people! It was all about Amnesty International, and here I was in India and not really aware.

I haven't been back since I left. I came back when I was eighteen, almost nineteen. I went when I was thirteen and a half.

You caught me in a bad year. The business opened nine years ago. I started working at the shop about six years ago. It's just a really rotten economy. Mostly we advertise with Austin Area Quilt Guild and our own mailing list—we have about eighteen hundred people on the list.

We are total hand-holders, and we're going to take the mystery out of it and make you comfortable. My dissatisfaction with our customers comes in waves. If we're making enough money for me to feed my family without worrying, I seem to not be bothered by a lot of bullshit that goes on. If the same customers come in and want a lot of attention and don't spend any money . . . [that bothers me. But] it's so counter to the way I was raised and so counter to

---

A friend entered a quilt in a show made with "antique-looking" off-white fabric for the background, with "antique-looking" embroidered Santas. She was told by the judge that quilts should be "clean" when entered into a show. Later the same quilt was entered into another show and won first prize. Another friend entered an antique strip-pieced quilt in a show and was told "the points don't even match." You never know about judges!

—Mary Nelle Figart, Bastrop, Texas

the way that I want to be, because I don't want to say, "Oh, she never spends any money in here . . ."—that's not it.

It's when it goes hand in hand with someone who's very needy and never spends any money in here. I always talk my way through it in a very neutral Buddhist way, where I'm like, "Put yourself in her shoes." And I always feel (a) guilty and then (b) much better once I get through it. On a day-to-day basis, sometimes you don't have time to do that and they irritate the shit out of you, and you're just like, at the end of the day, "Arghhhh, go away!"

Preelection [2004], that was the worst, catering to Republicans who want you to kiss their ass for like a month leading up to the election. I was feeling so, "I can't believe this is what I'm doing with my life. I should be changing the world." They'd find something on the bolt and say, "Where's the fat quarter of this?" And I'm like, "Do they look like they're filed?" If you look around here, there's piles of stuff everywhere. And I just want to go, "I don't know, but I'd be happy to cut you one." But I'm looking at the same basket of blue as she's looking at, and she doesn't see it . . . So that was hard, leading up to that point when I'm thinking I should be somewhere petitioning someone

---

I had just finished a quilt for my sister-in-law as a Christmas gift. It was a big, lap-size bargello quilt with a butterfly theme done in a rainbow of bright colors. At dinner on Christmas Eve, my husband asked her, "So, what kind of quilt would you want?"

Megan responded with, "Definitely something very traditional, maybe just red and white." I nearly blanched—but it was too late at that point. She was just gonna have to be happy with rainbows. The next morning when she got her quilt, she was gratifyingly surprised and just loved it. I think she was fine with the wild rainbow.

I've been fortunate. . . I've not made any irreparable mistakes. But there was one I did that was one of those that you piece and quilt all in one step, and I forgot to account for borders when I precut my batting and back—so I had to get kind of creative with the borders. I actually ended up doing the inner border with fabric-wrapped cord—so it looks thick, but actually didn't take up any space, which then allowed me to do a wide border on the outside. It turned out pretty well. —Robin Zaback, Cedar Park, Texas

---

or doing something important and I'm doing nothing important for no money.

When we bring up closing the shop and my husband, Matt, is like, "Okay, it's time to do it," and I'm like, "Okay"—and then I start to think about it, and I start to cry. There is a very deep root at this shop. It's like *Steel Magnolias*. You know, none of them really like each other, but they love each other deeply. It's the way I feel about the shop as a whole. I can't tell you how many mothers have broken down in tears in here because they've got four kids and they feel like they're going crazy, or someone who's just lost a son in a car wreck.

There's a very human thread, and I appreciate that immensely. It's just the day-to-day, you know, like the neurotic stuff you don't have time to dig through and see where it's coming from. You just have to deal with it, and that's really tedious. The books don't keep a lot of times. There's not time to do everything. We're scrambling constantly. It's hard to do.

On any given day, I sit down with some mother who's in here—and that's so important to me, that part of the shop where people come here because they're comfortable. They know they can bring their children here, and I'm not ever going to think twice if they pull something out and don't put it back. That's between them and their mom—she's going to figure it out; she'll work it out somewhere along the way. And they know that. They can't hurt anything in here that Liam hasn't already done somewhere along the road . . . Just sit down, have a cup of coffee.

What ends up happening is they relax, their kids relax. That whole frenetic, you know, "Don't do that! Don't do that!"—and the kids are doing it to push the buttons—that all goes away.

One customer, she has four kids. She's married to a backass redneck, but he's made a business for himself. She drives herself batty through trying to parent her kids, do what her therapist is telling her to do, what her husband is telling her to do. Basically everybody's telling her she's not good enough. Her therapist tells her she's doing it wrong. Her husband is basically saying, "You don't do anything," with no appreciation for her raising four children.

She comes in here with her three-and-a-half-year-old and he does what a three-and-a-half-year-old boy does, and she's yelling, "I'm talking to you!" and the voice goes up, up, up. And I just have said, "You know, he's fine. You know, I don't care. Use this as an opportunity to take him into a public place and do what you need to do." And she says, "Does that mean if I need to smack him . . ." And I say, "No," because I don't think you do. My dad used to take us to a Mexican restaurant as our trial restaurant. He used to take us there to teach us manners. He didn't take us to Fonda San Miguel and expect us to act well. He took us to El Azteca, and they didn't give a shit if he's dragging us out to the car screaming because we did bad behavior.

I told her that story and said, "See what happens if you just kind of observe and watch him, and then if he crosses a line . . . but not feel like he's crossing every line in here."

It's easy from the outside to say, "Just come sit with me for a minute." That happens once every couple days with somebody, and it has nothing to do with quilting. It has to do with they were attracted to quilting, so they came in here. They stayed because they were welcome. That's brought us lots of different kinds of people.

I get it from my mom. I got it from watching her. We hold each other up so much. We have issues, don't get me wrong. But there's a very deep root of love there. People come here and spend money because we've done this for years. We've sat down and talked and consoled and empathized. I feel like we're kind of in this trap of having to do that and stop what we're doing [cutting fabric].

People will drive all the way down here from wherever to come here, probably not to buy what they need—because we only have like nine hundred bolts—but on the chance they might find something that we can help them make work for whatever they're doing, because we'll talk to them. And they don't have to ask. We'll ask them. We're not going to treat them like they're stupid.

If I had to put it in a nutshell, it's a very difficult balance between feeling that a lot of my heart is in the shop and it doesn't make enough money. The root of all the problems that I have, the emotional issues, it all comes back to cash flow. You have to make a certain amount of money to pay the rent and keep the lights on, and some months we don't make enough money to do that. Then I'm frustrated. I'm frustrated with my kids because my brain's thinking about one thing, and they're jabbering about something else. And it's not about that they're seven and three, but it comes back to, "Oh shit, how are we going to pay the rent and not have the phone cut off?" If we had a solid cash flow that could be counted on, then I would run this shop forever.

14

Those Who Can, Do;
Those Who Can, Also Teach

I met Hella Wagner when I gave a reading to a group gathered for a holiday celebration for the Friends of the Austin Public Library in December 2003. Hella is a great example of how I stumbled across many of the wonderful people I interviewed for this book. She came up to me to talk about my reading. I mentioned in passing that I was researching a book on quilting, only to discover that there I was, once again, standing in the company of a great quilter.

It took me a year before I managed to get to her house, and immediately she put me at ease. Where did I want to sit? Was I right-handed or left (so she could position a small table for my mug)? What sort of tea did I drink? Hella is a detail person, a fact displayed not only in her hostessing but also in her quilts.

Hanging on one wall was a gorgeous square-within-a-square quilt (hand-pieced and hand-quilted). There was also an abundance of needlepoint, much of it done by one of her daughters. On another wall there was a small Christmas quilt that was so intricately detailed it was breathtaking. Scrutinizing it, I realized I could finally understand what was going on here. Two years before I couldn't tell a sweatshop quilt from a work of art.

Now I observed this small quilt, how it was pieced together, each piece tiny, many of them curved, with itty-bitty, completely even hand stitches. I'm pretty sure my jaw was hanging open.

Hella's house felt so good, as if she'd put a good deal of thought into every inch of every room. In fact, this is exactly the truth. I'm not sure if she brought her quilting sensibility to creating her serene nest, or if perhaps these skills had always been with her and she applied them to her quilting. Either way, Hella clearly has a sense of what she wants. And so once again, I came to talk about quilting and found myself being inspired in other areas too.

Hella was divorced after thirty-five years of marriage. At the end of her marriage she had to essentially start her life from scratch. Scrimping and saving finally afforded her a cozy little house, which she then updated and furnished to her precise specifications. Her beautiful collection of wooden figurines from East Germany, where she grew up (she moved to the United States in 1969). Her new hardwood floors. And, most importantly, her current, ongoing project—her garden. Hella talked to me about her strength, her joys, her adventures in horticulture, and, of course, her quilting, including why she no longer enters competitions and her past life of teaching quilting.

"In '78 we were in Lubbock, and a quilt store opened and they had free demonstration sessions. And I went to all of them, and before the last session, I signed up for my first class and that was the beginning of everything. Then I worked on the quilt. A year after that, my husband got transferred to Austin. They were so sweet at the quilt store in Lubbock. They found out all about the Austin Area Quilt Guild for me, and as soon as they found out where we were going to be, they told me where the closest quilting bee was. That must have been my very first phone call when we got a phone in the house.

The quilting community is a great community. No matter who you are, they take you in, just like that. They're a bunch of very nice people. Of course there are some people that you don't get along too well with in any group, but most of the people are just wonderful.

I dropped out when I had problems with going through the divorce, and I needed to go to Germany for an extended period of time because my mother had cancer. Then I was busy trying to make a living from nothing and didn't go back because I couldn't even afford the membership fee at that point. I was for years in a quilting bee. It was fun. Then I had to go back to work full-time, and my quilting bee met from ten till two on Mondays, and that went by the wayside—if you have to make a living, that's out. And I tried to find another one that was meeting in the evening. Just couldn't really find the right group that I was comfortable with.

I've always grown up with needlework. My mother was a great teacher with the patience of a saint. Growing up in Eastern Germany, there wasn't much that you could do, but she was always able to rustle up something. She's kept all my little needlework things. When I go back visiting, then I pull out the stuff and say, "Look at this . . . I remember that."

I used to have a huge stash, but I'm not doing much in the quilting because of gardening. Another year I can see—another year, maybe two—then I will have my garden at maintenance level. Then I can go back to my quilting. My friends were very stumped when after I bought the house, I dropped just about all the sewing projects, and it was just coming home and going outside. I had a vision of what I wanted to do with that garden. It's the same thing [as quilting]—you're just working with a different medium. You have a big piece of fabric that you buy at the store, and I think you can probably relate that to that crabby old lawn I had out front.

Putting in the different pieces of my landscape in the front is like putting a quilt panel together. Designing the quilt, you need to think about the covers. In gardening you need to think more about the three-dimensional effect than

---

Quilting is relaxing and aesthetically satisfying. It trains me in persistence, and there's always something new to try when I get bored.

I made this quilt for an ex using just the extra triangles and squares from a class I'd taught. It took about six hours to lay out all the pieces on the kitchen floor, rearranging them until it looked good. Then I sewed the top in a single 20-hour stretch. When I was most of the way done with the quilting, I discovered that I'd rotated one block 90 degrees, so it wasn't symmetrical with the four other analogous blocks. For months after that, I'd invite people to find the mistake—and not a single person could see it until I pointed it out.

—Kate Walker, Austin, Texas

in quilting. You can't put a big heavy six-foot bush right in front next to the sidewalk. I had one of those—you back out of your driveway you can't see a thing. So that had to go.

I have several ribbons on quilts I've made. It depends totally on the judges you get. The judges are supposed to be impartial, but if you've been around the quilting community for a while, you know that this judge, for instance, would prefer conventional quilts, this judge likes art quilts, and so if you have a conventional quilt and you get a judge who likes art quilts, you get a lousy rating.

I've been a judge myself, and I know that you're influenced by your likes and dislikes. There is just no way around it—it's very judgmental. I said, "I don't want to make a quilt to please somebody else. I make a quilt because I happen to like this particular one." And that's when I decided, "Okay. I'll put my quilt in a show, yes. But no, I will not have it judged anymore." I want to do a quilt that pleases me. Only if I'm planning to give a quilt to somebody else, then I will find out what that person likes. But if that is a quilt I'm doing because I want to do it, I don't give a damn about a judge.

I don't machine-quilt. I machine-piece—if I feel like. People will say I'm a very traditional quilter, and that probably fits the category best. I like the old designs. I like the looks of the old quilts. And I like just sitting here and piecing; it is so relaxing. For me, sitting at the sewing machine is still hard work. Just sitting on the couch and piecing—I get a book on tape or I have my CDs playing—I can *totally* forget about the time. I always hand-quilt in an eighteen-inch hoop. I sit on the couch cross-legged, and I rest the hoop on my legs. I've caught myself falling asleep, because when I woke up, it was one o'clock in the morning and it was like, "Maybe I should be going to bed. I have to go to work in the morning."

Let me show you this one over here. This is a calendar, see. I used some of the patterns and redesigned some of the others. I never follow the patterns exactly. They're all machine-pieced, and these blocks are machine-quilted. This was a class that I taught at the Bernina Sewing Center. When I was teaching at Bernina, three stores, you needed to make three samples of everything. People signing up for the classes want to see the real thing. They don't want to just look at the pictures. So I have one, my mom has one, and one of my daughters has one.

How long did I teach? I think about six, seven years at Bernina. I taught adult education [too]. I'll show them the right way, but I will not critique any-body too badly. I learned my lesson early on. We were doing place mats just to get people started. It was a very beginning class.

One lady, points didn't mean anything to her, that they could not be cut off didn't mean anything to her, that seams were supposed to match didn't mean anything to her either. So she came, at the second class—she came with a place mat that nothing matched, and she was so happy, so exuberant that I told myself, "Don't criticize." I said, "How do you feel about it?" She said, "Oh, I love it! And my daughter's all excited about it, and I'm going to make three more so she has a set of four!"

I set the bar high, but I will let everybody work at their own level. If they're happy with it, I'm happy with it.

I never timed my quilts. The only time frames I've put on the quilts was when I was teaching, that I had to have . . . a month before the class was sup-posed to start, the samples had to be in the store. This is the deadline you have to keep if you want people to sign up for your class, because they won't sign up from a piece of paper.

[My square-in-a-square quilt] is a total scrap quilt. In my scrap quilts I need some coordination. I can't do totally without, so the black coordinates it and then I kind of stay in a square within a square, and I stay within a color within a square.

I tack up a flannel sheet on the wall, and then I lay out my blocks on my wall and they stick to it, so you don't have to pin them. And then I'll go by and I'll look at it, and there's one block "Oh God, that shouldn't be there"—so I take it and move it someplace else. So if I have passed that quilt for a couple of weeks and nothing bothers me anymore, then I'll sew it together.

Her advice:

" Do what you like. You can ask for help with color. In the beginning, lots of quilters need help with color. Don't go and ask for help at Wal-Mart. Go and find an independent dealer, and ask for help there. Or join the quilt guild. You might get more help than you really want.

15

Sewing on the River (and Everywhere Else)

Eighteen years ago when I lived in Knoxville, Tennessee, I met a man named Billy, who asked me if I knew what a penny tasted like. Of course I did. Then he wanted to know when was the last time I put a penny in my mouth. I had no idea. His point, I think, was that pennies have such a distinct taste we never forget them and that at some point, probably when we're very little and putting everything in our mouths, we experience that unforgettable flavor.

I can't think of anyone I know who wouldn't get an immediate mental picture upon hearing the word "quilt." Even if they'd never seen one in real life. Or if they weren't around quilts with any regularity. Quilts, like the taste of pennies, leave an indelible impression.

I'm trying to remember my first quilt—the first time I encountered one. Honestly, I have no clue when that was. I'm not from a quilting family, and so, though I like to imagine being wrapped up in one on some childhood visit to one of my grandmothers—Murphy Mom-Mom and Peachy Mom-Mom—in South Philadelphia, I seriously doubt any scene like that actually occurred.

It is entirely possible that Elise Judy first brought quilts into my life. Her daughter, Paula, was my dormmate and then my roommate in college in Tampa, Florida, in the early eighties. This was one of those situations everyone should be lucky enough to have—a tossed-together situation where you meet someone with whom you become lifelong friends.

Paula and I roomed together on and off after college too. She moved to Texas first and then encouraged me to follow her, which I did, seemingly on a whim (though now I think maybe fate had a hand). Over the years, I grew close with Paula's family too. I've been on numerous canoe excursions with her father, who, at eighty, still likes to shoot the rapids. I've hung out with her parents at their summer cabin in Franklin, North Carolina, one of two places where Elise belongs to quilting groups. The other group is in her hometown, Fort Lauderdale.

And all along the way, without even realizing it until now, there were Elise's quilts. She's made twenty quilts in the two decades I've know her. And, to hear her tell it, she's got plans for plenty more

" All the women in my family have sewed, knitted, or been in some form of making things from material or yarn. It was natural that I took it up, although I am the first quilter, I believe. I remember my mother's sister describing how she and the other young women of her time used to create lingerie and other such things for each other around Christmastime and how the gifts had a particular meaning since they were made with love and care.

I think about twenty-five years ago I saw an article in a magazine having to do with making a bear's-claw quilt, so I did that all by hand. It's pieced. All of the quilts I've made are pieced. I haven't tried appliqué yet, but I will. It had thirty-six squares. And I would take one square with me when we went driving somewhere long distance or canoeing somewhere. Or when I was waiting for airplanes—it's very good to have a little handwork to do. I was very pleased with the way that came out.

I think my biggest mistake was to use cheap material on my first quilt. I have little by little had to replace every patch in this quilt as the fabric wore out. As it was my first quilt, I am very attached to it, which is why I bother.

Every time I make one, I see other pictures and other designs, and I just have to try them. I'm backed up probably about six designs right now. I've made twenty quilts in all.

I do the quilting by hand, but sometimes I do the piecing by machine. I

Wendy Judy Sherrard and her daughter, Sara, holding up a quilt made for
them by Wendy's mom and Sara's grandmother, Elise Judy. The quilt is made
of African themed fabrics in a pattern called Spider Web. Photo courtesy of Elise Judy.

have a quilting frame that's maybe about three feet by four feet all made out
of PVC pipe, and you can take it down and put it up. So when I have one on
the frame, I put it up. And I always have one on the frame. When I sit at my
quilting frame, I have to sit high. If I sit on the end of the bed, that's about
right. So the quilting frame is always at the end of the bed.

The group in North Carolina, which is sort of a subgroup of a guild out there, doesn't make the quilt tops, but they do the quilting of the layers, and they charge for it and the money goes to a scholarship fund. Every year they give three or four scholarships to local high school students. They don't amount to a big sum, but every little bit helps.

My other group in Fort Lauderdale hooked up with Habitat for Humanity, and every family that goes into a new Habitat home is presented with a quilt from this group. We use donated fabric and they're very scrappy scrap quilts, but it's amazing how pretty they all turn out, as random as they are—we make the most elegant quilts from the sorriest bunch of fabrics you have ever seen. Some have their sewing machines and sew; some design; some cut the pieces. Everyone seems to know what they are doing, and the whole thing just falls together.

The families know they're going to get one, and it's very important to them that they get one. And it's very important that it's pretty—as pretty as the other ones. [She laughs.] They have a little ceremony. Usually in Broward County they build in neighborhoods, like they build five or six homes all together on one street, and usually they'll have a dedication of those homes. And the people get the keys, and they also get these quilts and they're very happy to have them.

The group in Fort Lauderdale is black women and white women, and that's the only quilters' guild I've been a part of that's mixed in that way. The more we work together, the more we see we have in common—a nice group of women. The one that sort of ran it when I first joined was a woman from South Africa—that's sort of an odd little sidenote.

The next in command is a woman from Germany named Rita. She has lived all over the world, and she has a marvelous sense of design. I kind of follow patterns and repeat what I see. This woman can take things, and she is so creative and one thing leads to another, and you really have something unusual at the end. Then the black women—one of them is retired Post Office. The last meeting, Rita brought her daughter, who happened to be in town from Seattle. She's a professor at the University of Washington. And Bernice—that's the retired postal worker—brought her daughter, who's working on a doctorate. It was kind of fun to have two people with their daughters there.

My group in Franklin, they're mostly even older than I am. Most of them have been quilting for years and years and years. But it's nice. I like just sitting with a group of women and working. I probably don't have a lot in common with them, but you always have something in common with almost anyone. You talk about this, and you talk about that. It was a nest of Democrats in Fort Lauderdale, but in Franklin I don't think so, so we kind of avoided the subject.

Rosemary Kimsey's shop [in Franklin]—it's an old family in town. The fabric salesmen come by her place. They know where she is, and she has just never seen a fabric she could refuse, so she buys them all. And she runs the shop on a country road in the middle of nowhere. It happens to be her deceased mother's old house. And it is absolutely full of fabric in every room— the living room, the bedrooms—and yet, I took three fabrics out there which I had purchased the year before, and I needed a little more. I said, "Is it at all possible to get a little more of each one of these?" And she did it. She went— out of all of those thousands and thousands of bolts—to the right place and got it.

I think another thing she does is have a connection with some ladies out in the country, and they make quilt tops. Now she's taught her husband to quilt—that's another thing—so he quilts. It's not the best quilting you'll ever see. She sells quilts, and she sells all sorts of things for quilts. She lives behind this old house that's full of fabric. They farm and raise cows, I guess for milk. This particular day we went out there, the calves were bawling because they were being weaned, so she was kind of between me and the calves and she jumps from one subject to the other.

The guild in North Carolina is very large. I don't even know how large. They must have at least fifty members. Those of us who quilt meet every Friday and Monday. It's usually from six to ten of us at the most. Usually we meet in a little building that belongs to the city of Franklin—they give us a room there. We have two very big frames up and quilts and all kinds of stuff.

My favorite part of quilting? I like every part of it, really. I go through pattern books and look at patterns. I'm backed up—there's so many I want to try. Well, I don't like cutting out pieces, I will say that. That's a very annoying part of it. I usually use scissors. Unless you've got even squares—then a rotary cutter. I use both. For borders a rotary cutter is very good and fast.

I love the piecing, and I like the quilting too. I used not to like the quilting. When I started to like it is when I got to doing this quilting with the women in North Carolina. Now I really like it. I find it relaxing to sit and do that. It's just is a nice way to get together and have a little conversation. Every Friday we go in at nine o'clock, and we usually break around eleven thirty and go to lunch. Then we come back and quilt till two or two thirty. Then every Monday we only quilt in the morning usually—say, nine till twelve.

My very two favorites [in North Carolina are] Myra and Joy. They're well into their eighties, and they're in there every week. Doing Mondays and Fridays, we probably take three months per quilt top. It depends how much quilting is on it. Some have a lot; some have a little. The people who make the top can choose the quilting pattern, but they usually leave it to us. Joyce is usually the expert on that.

We all baste it. We have a big Ping-Pong table—we clip it or tape it. When I do one of mine, we don't even have anyplace big enough to baste it. I usually go up to the recreation center and ask them if they'll let me use it when no one else is using it. But then I have to put it on the floor and tape it down.

I go at it alone. I'm a renegade. Don't want anyone telling me I'm doing anything wrong! This hobby is supposed to be for pleasure and leisure, not evaluation, eh?

I'm a control freak. I like to be able to do something that I can stay with until the end. That kind of control isn't possible in a typical corporate career, so I started quilting. This is a hobby where I can take something from start to finish and totally have a say in what is going on. I love the feeling of a completed project. (Whether anyone likes it or not isn't the goal—the goal is only if I like it!) Once finished, I immediately start working on something else.

One of my very first quilts was a hand-tied quilt, made three years ago. I didn't have any experience whatsoever with this type of quilt, but I figured, "Hmmm . . . I'm a smart girl. So you tie the quilt together with yarn and a big ol' needle? What's the big deal?" Well, I wasn't aware of the tools available to me in the "wide world of quilting," so I used a big upholstery needle and my teeth. Yes, my teeth were used to pull this rather large needle through the fabric and batting! I now sport a beautiful straight front tooth (straight 'cause I just paid five thousand dollars for braces a year ago) with a rather large indentation on the tooth, courtesy of pulling this needle through. Not such a smart girl after all. But one with pretty teeth (minus the indentation).
—Gabriela Voss, Coppell, Texas

And at my age it's not too easy to scramble around the floor and do it, but I don't know any other way to do it.

We've tried all kinds of things [to mark the quilting pattern]. It's very hard to find something that will really wash out but will stay there long enough. On a dark fabric I like to use a white charcoal pencil. That's very good— you go into an art store and ask for a charcoal pencil that's white, which you wouldn't think there would be such a thing but there is. And we try those blue fabric markers. What I've been using lately is just a sliver of soap; that's very good on dark fabrics. Whatever you've used at the sink and it's too small to be anything other than annoying to you, that's just right.

When I started having grandchildren, I thought, "I'll make each of them a Raggedy Ann and Andy doll," which is something I've made a lot. That didn't suit [my daughter] Wendy—she wanted a quilt. I made Zachary a quilt, and of course I had to make the other two quilts, too. So among the twenty quilts are three for the grandchildren.

I made one quilt for the daughter of a friend of mine in California. Her mother, who was my close friend when I started working, died. Her daughter had some of her clothes left, and she wanted them made into a quilt. I made one for Paula, and she has it. And I made one for Wendy out of all African fabrics—that has a lot of quilting on it. Other than that, I'm making one for my sister right now. It's on the frame. All the others out of the twenty are mine.

The thing about quilting is you can cover up mistakes. The expert quilter in the quilting guild in Franklin makes frequent mistakes. Now, she's very good—she's won, in regional contests, ribbons of all kinds. She makes all these mistakes, but she appliqués a little bird or flower over the mistake.

I think the best thing a quilter can do is to be patient and not rush things along. There is no hurry. I am a leisurely quilter, and yet I have more quilts completed than I will ever be able to use. It is good to enjoy the process as it unfolds before you. Take advantage of the little surprises that develop. There is nothing so satisfying as to create something in peaceful surroundings with a group of other women.

1 6

Manly Quilt Man

When necessary, Bob Ruggiero can effortlessly break into a flawless imper-
sonation of a radio announcer or game show host. I first met Bob at IQF
2002. He is the go-to man for press credentials for the show, the guy
standing there at the proverbial red velvet rope, determining which writers
merit a green ribbon and all that implies.

Endearing myself to Bob meant earning certain privileges. A press pass
equals free snacks and drinks served up in a room that can be used to interview subjects. The pressroom also provides a little respite when one's
feet are about to fall off or when one just wants to look out from a second-
floor porthole down over the entire floor of the quilt show. Best of all,
though, pressroom access means Bob access, and Bob, it must be noted,
is a very, very funny man.

I can't tell you precisely how funny he is, because Bob—at least with
this reporter—may say something witty and hilarious and earthy, and
then immediately follow up this witticism with the finishing comment:
"Off the record."

But trust me, even though he doesn't quilt, Bob has seen and knows
more than most of us have seen and know when it comes to all things

quilting. I love racing up to see him upon arriving at the show, certain he will say something along these lines in that smooth, professional voice of his: "Well, things are very exciting this year, Spike. This could be the largest show ever!"

And I, in turn, will feel an irresistible urge to beg him to do his "rolling luggage announcement" for me, an announcement he makes about fifty billion times during the course of each IQF weekend. Bob, obliging me and pretending to be speaking to an audience of thousands over a PA system, will say, "There's no rolling luggage allowed on the show floor due to safety and security reasons. Thank you."

Bob is fond of making the following claim, which I have been forced to abbreviate, courtesy of his "off the record" demands regarding some of the claim: "In order to regain my masculinity after spending two weeks with 99 percent females, I go to the woods. I turn on sports even though I don't watch sports. I'll tinker around with the car even though I barely know how to inflate a tire."

I've been interviewing Bob informally over the years, but in the fall of 2004, I actually hazarded the labyrinth that is the Houston highway system to pay him a visit at Quilts, Inc., which is the mother ship, so to speak, the umbrella organization that produces the International Quilt Festival.

My real goal that day was the Holy Grail of interviews, a private audience with Quilting Queen Bee (or shall I say Bee Queen?) Karey Bresenhan. Karey was sick, which was unfortunate for her but turned out to be a blessing for me. I used my allotted time to quiz Bob, who had a lot to say that surprised me, about how he came to be a permanent member of the organization and the moment that has (thus far) moved him most.

" I do need to preface our little tour of the office by saying we are still unpacking a lot of boxes from the show—our walls are usually all decorated by quilts, but a lot of them were on display during the show. But you'll get to see the epicenter of where all the shows begin. I've gotta tell you, of all the offices in this building, we have the finest door [he gestures to a leaded glass French door inlaid with a big Q].

Here we have our library. We use it as a reference library. We have thousands of books and magazines. This isn't even the whole collection. Mostly it's for reference for the staff.

Karey decided to have a pin for each show. This is the actual collection of every pin we've ever done, going back to the very first ones. People collect these things. You go on eBay, and people are selling them. The years we sell out, people freak out—they don't know where they can get one. Literally, when people buy a ticket, the first thing they say when they come through the door is, "Where are the pins?" They go straight to the booth.

Now, if you pre-enroll for one of our classes, you get one of these pins automatically. Some of them you only get for volunteering. Some of them you get for being a teacher's pet. The people who guard the quilts get a special one. All of our overseas shows have their special ones. We produce, every two years, a Quilt Expo in Europe in different European cities. We've done nine of them so far—Germany, France, Spain, Austria.

This is our special exhibits department. Vicki coordinates with getting them here, getting them hung. It's like a major military operation. This year we had over two thousand different pieces of art. Vicki and her assistant had to coordinate getting them all in, checking them all out, and deciding where they go on the showroom floor.

We're going to be working on food leftover from the show for some time. We have a lot of low-carb people this year, so we have low-carb candy bars.

This is my eighth year here. My temporary job became my career. I figured I would work here for a couple of years and move on. I was a newspaper editor in Georgia. I was there for five years, and my girlfriend—now my wife—was living with me. And she was very homesick, and she said, "Let's move back to Houston."

I had some reservations about it because we're both from here. I said, "Okay, if we move back to Houston, I've got to have a writing job. I'm not going to go be a manager of a Blockbuster or Sound Warehouse or flip burgers or anything." I'm a graduate of UT [the University of Texas at Austin]. I got the *UT Alumni Newsletter* and was looking through the want ads, and there was this mysterious ad for a writer. Very skimpy on the details. It just said, "Respond to Q Incorporated."

If it had said "Quilts Incorporated," I would've never answered that ad. But I answered it. And I had a couple of phone interviews, and they flew me down here for the interview, flew me back down to see the show, and then offered me the job. At that point I was thinking, "It's a writing job, and you know, who knows?" I'm still waiting for *Rolling Stone* to open up their Houston offices, but that's not going to happen.

The day they flew me in, the *Houston Chronicle* happened to run a story on Quilt Festival, so I knew it was going to be sort of a big deal. But when I walked in for the first time and saw it, I couldn't believe it. I spent hours roaming and roaming the aisles. At this point, I don't think I'd accepted the job yet. Being the journalism major, I thought, "I gotta find out." So I wandered up and down the hallways trying to get a grip on what I might be getting myself into.

Initially it was kind of a weird gig, being in quilts. I have the same suppositions anybody had—grandma on the back porch. A lot of times I wouldn't tell my friends what I did or I'd couch it in very vague terms: "Oh, I'm the, uh, writer for a company that produces shows that travel the world . . ."—things like that.

Eight years really changed my mind about it. I've gotten to know that this really is an art form and it's a livelihood for people and it's a thriving hobby, and that [it] stretches worldwide. It's a huge industry.

I have buddies who come to see the show in Houston, and they can't believe it. The mouth always drops open. People lose control of their chin when they walk in. The ligaments all disappear, and I think what impresses people most is just the scope of it. When you walk into either the George Brown or the Stephens Center in Chicago—anywhere where we have our shows—the first thing people can't believe is that it's this massive. There are so many booths selling things and so many quilts on display.

The second thing is, the color hits people. All these quilts on display are all different colors. It's like this sensory *pop*! I think that's what bowls people over most, even more than the crowds.

There was one time that I got choked up. I think a lot of people in this office would give the same answer—I think it was the September 11 quilts. That show—that's a whole fascinating story in itself. September 11 happened, and people were just freaked out. Karey was monitoring one of the online chats for quilters and said. "Any quilts you make about September 11, I'll display them."

So we were expecting about fifty quilts to come in, because the show was only six weeks after September 11. But we had to cut it off at, like, three hundred. The most emotional thing is just walking and seeing these quilts on display. Some were patriotic, one has Osama Bin Laden, some are really just touching, and people are just openly crying.

Some of those quilts made me choke up too. The one that really, really—at this point I was a new father of a little girl—one of these quilts is called *And the Door Never Opened*. It's a quilt with a little girl at the day care, waiting for her mother to pick her up, and obviously her mother was in the Twin Towers. I just started crying. I never thought something like that would affect me. But I just had a daughter. That one was a little rough to see.

Outside of myself, just seeing all these people come together for this exhibit . . . And it wasn't just Americans—we have people from all over the world coming to these shows. These people were stopping at these quilts and reading the artists' statements, because that was also a part of it. Each person wrote a little bit about how they made the quilt and what it meant to them. One woman who lives near the Pentagon made a big quilt of the shadow of the airplane passing over her house.

That [exhibit] was probably the most touching, emotional moment that the show ever put on.

I went on a mission trip to Samoa. The fabric there was very inexpensive, but the prints and fabric were beautiful. I brought a lot of fabric back with me. It has been sitting in my closet for about three years.

When I started quilting, my eleven-year-old daughter, Ali, went to quilting classes with me. She wanted to learn to sew, and make a quilt of her own. The teacher was thrilled to have a child in the class. All the ladies just fawned over her and encouraged her, and even taught her to crochet. Ali came with the intention of making a quilt with surfboards. She wanted to redo her bedroom to look like a beach house.

One night we were at my sister's, and my nephew had a new spread on his bed, with surfboards! Ali asked my sister where she had gotten the fabric. That's right, the fabric was from me. I went home, and we found another piece with surfboards. We have been planning and purchasing ever since.

This week we put together the first square. The quilt is going to be darling. But the best part has been that Ali and I have something in common. We look forward to sneaking away to the loft and working on our projects. We shop together and plan together. It has made us very close.

—Barbie Gopperton, Mesa, Arizona

17

One Quilt, One Love

Debra Armstrong lives in Lockhart, a little town with a population of about eleven thousand, thirty miles south of Austin. I heard of Debra the way I heard of a lot of the quilters I interviewed. I was out at a nonquilting event, and I began talking about my interest in the topic. My friend Anna Borne approached me and strongly advised that I invite myself to see a Victorian crazy quilt Debbie had made.

After talking to Debbie on the phone about how her quilt came to be, I made an appointment to visit her home, a two-story glorious Victorian built in 1892, which she and her husband bought in 1995 and spent five years renovating. Debbie says they had no idea what they were getting into, and the endeavor was very much an example of ignorance equaling bliss.

Her sweat equity was my great fortune, as was the fact that the quilt in question happened to be upstairs in a back bedroom. Which meant I got a tour of the place on the way to see the quilt. I told Debbie that being at her house reminded me of something a photographer once told me, when we were on assignment in a resort area, looking at some really hideous but incredibly expensive houses. Bob, the photographer, said, "There's a wide gulf between wealth and taste."

Debbie assures me she lives on a budget, but if you could put a dollar amount on taste, she would be a billionaire. She and her husband are collectors, and they like to display groupings of their collected items throughout their home. On the kitchen wall, for example, is his collection of plates featuring pictures of Texas Methodist churches from the forties and fifties. Who even knew such a thing existed? On another wall, a huge collection of bright Mexican masks. In one bedroom, dozens of sock monkeys, some with "their arms loved off," as Debbie put it. Everywhere I turned, I was overwhelmed, in the best sense of the word, by the great things collected and the wonderful way these collections were displayed.

And then came . . . The Quilt. I helped Debbie pull back the white sheet the quilt stays hidden beneath to minimize dust collection. There it was, and I was not disappointed. Done in mostly dark silks, with some outstanding moments of light, bordered in black velvet, it was tied at the corners, which were done in brassy silk. The details are barely describable. At first you don't even realize there are individual blocks. With a number of pieces set at an angle, the whole quilt does at first appear to have a crazy nonpattern to it.

But stare long enough and things start popping out. A mother and baby. A bluebonnet. A calla lily. A catfish. A tatted Christmas tree. A woman's hand. The bluebird of happiness. And hearts and more hearts.

One thing I most liked about talking quilts with Debbie is that she proved, once again, that every quilter has a unique story. In her case, although she has made a couple of other quilts—both smaller and featuring redwork embroidery—this one big quilt was a project unto itself. It was not the start of Debbie's embarking on a long life of multiple quilt creation. It was not the trigger that sent her into a stash-buying frenzy. This is a quilt that just sort of came to her. She knew she had to do it. She did it. That's enough. Which isn't to say she's done with quilting, only that she hasn't felt instantly compelled to start another and another.

Every quilt I saw along the way inspired me somehow. This quilt inspired me with its artistry. It also inspired me with the idea that, even if I ever make only one or two quilts in my lifetime, what counts is what I put into that work.

Here, Debbie talks about her quilt:

"It was one of those things—who doesn't admire Victorian crazy quilts, right? They're the most beautiful things. Every time I saw one at a quilt show or out for sale, I thought, "You know, one day I'm going to have one of those, because I want to have one and use it." Okay, well, the reality is if you could ever afford one, you couldn't actually really use it, because it's not practical. They've stayed in such good shape for a reason—people put them away in the cedar chest and keep them because they're not practical to use.

I finally got to the point where I said to myself, "You know, you can do this. You know how to embroider, and that's the primary thing that crazy quilts have going for it is the massive amounts of embroidery on the really nice ones." So I just sat down, and, you know, you work on them in squares. So I just started making squares, and basically it was kind of a catharsis. It's a life quilt. I just went through, and each square that I did, I didn't necessarily think about it in advance, but as I started on it, I started getting ideas for . . . "Okay, it's Valentine's Day. I'm going to do a Valentine's square." Or "It's

Debra Armstrong's *Victorian Crazy Quilt*, photographed on the porch of her Victorian home in Lockhart, Texas. Photo by Eli Durst.

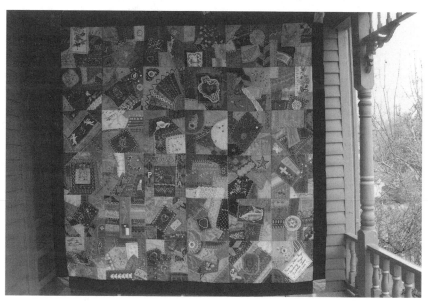

Detail of Debra Armstrong's *Victorian Crazy Quilt*. Photo by Eli Durst.

Detail of Debra Armstrong's *Victorian Crazy Quilt*. Photo by Eli Durst.

New Year's of the millennium. I'm going to do a New Year's square." Or my marriage. I got kind of prompted by whatever it was I was working on at the moment on the square. It kind of came forth out of me.

It took me a year to do it. I started in 1999; I finished in 2000. At the end of it I felt like I had pretty much gotten everything into it that I wanted—everything that was important to me in my life, everything important to me in my life in Texas, childhood things. Just everything I could think of that was important to me, I put into this quilt. So in terms of doing another one like this particular one, I don't think I could unless I wait another fifty years and have enough life experience where I could do another one.

I had made small things, more traditional quilting. I don't have the patience to do traditional quilting. I think it's way too repetitive. I've done other crazy quilt things. I've done a baby quilt and a Davy Crockett quilt, and I've done other quilt things. But one of this magnitude, I don't know that I could do it again.

I made it to go on my bed, which is a queen size. After all is said and done, I can't use it, because it's not practical to use, so it's on the guest room bed, which is a double. It's heavy because of all the embellishment on it. It would be spectacular on the wall, and I did have it in a quilt show in Lockhart there for a while, and it was hanging up and it was really beautiful. But the weight of it may be too much for it to bear [if it were hanging for a long period].

I am caregiver to my invalid mother since 1999. I was becoming very depressed because it is a very hard watching someone fading away from you and there is nothing you can do to stop it. One day my husband suggested I take a quilting class. It was the very best therapy I could have had.

There are still times when I don't have the time to quilt for days at a time, but when I do finally get back to my sewing machine, I lose myself in the work of making quilts. I have even figured out a way for my mother to help. She is wheelchair bound and isn't able to do much, never having had any hobbies. She now gets her name on most of my quilts as the one who removes all the basting pins at the finish. Together we make fun quilts for all her great-grandchildren, grandchildren, relatives, and friends. It makes her feel useful again.

—Susan Emge Milliner, Cedar Park, Texas

I worked on it every night. I probably put at least a couple of hours a night. And then on the weekends. You know, it's one of those things that once you get into, you hate to put it down. Up to that point I'm very lucky. I didn't have anything horrible that I put into the quilt. It's all good stuff. Everything's done by hand, except when I sewed the squares together, I did that by machine, and then I embellished over the seams—you can't tell it's done by machine. I didn't quilt it, because crazy quilts don't get quilted—they get tied. It's tied in the corners. I was on the floor, and it was almost harder than doing the thing, because it's so big and being on the floor and trying to tie it, and I didn't have any space to put it other than the floor.

I loved every minute of it—you do get stuck constantly—but I love it. That's why I was able to finish it, and I kind of missed it when I was done. That's why I continue to do other projects on a smaller scale. I really think there was some sort of inspiration going on. It all just flowed so easily. There wasn't anything that was [unpleasant] about it.

I never put it down. I just worked on it constantly because I knew the way that I am with projects sometimes—that if I put it down, I'm not likely to go back to it. But the beauty of crazy quilts [is], you finish a square, you get to the point where you say, "Okay, this is it," [and] you move onto something else. So you're constantly inspired. You're not doing the same thing over and over again.

Probably the one I did of my marriage, that one's got a special meaning. I put my handprint and my wedding ring, and I put little sayings around it like, "With this ring I thee wed" and just little stuff that doesn't mean anything to anybody but me. My quilt is very folk-arty—that's the appeal of crazy quilts to me. You see a lot of modern crazy quilts that are just too cutesy and too overdone and too preplanned, I think, and mine doesn't have that. Like I say, each square was a different inspiration, and I'm a big fan of folk art anyway.

I like people to see it. God knows I try and show it off anytime anybody shows the slightest bit of interest. My husband, who's a great advocate of mine . . . there was a quilt show in one of the churches, and he said, "You gotta do this." So he contacted them and got it in and hung up there, and it was really pleasing to see, if I do say so.

18

Bee Queen

In the quilting world, rarely if ever does Karey Bresenhan need an introduction. Most everyone knows Karey as the head of Quilts, Inc., and, as such, the head of the International Quilt Festival, the largest annual quilt event in the world. As it happened—coincidence or fate, you decide—Karey came to be the last person I interviewed for this book. That wasn't how I planned it, but our busy schedules dictated that this is how history would have things go. For me, there was something poetic to this timing. And while I certainly won't ever come close to having the sort of knowledge Karey holds regarding everything quilt-related, I confess I was nearly giddy when we spoke, simply because I could actually understand what the hell she was talking about.

So what if I still hadn't finished that first quilt yet. I had been so educated by so many wonderful quilters along the way, not only did I know the basic glossary words like "thread" and "stitch," but I even knew the difference between machine-sewn and hand-sewn. I knew some of the big players in the world of competitive quilting. I knew something. I think that felt good, not so much from a bragging standpoint, but more like I was finally prepared to eat dinner at the adults' table and not totally fumble during the conversation.

Karey wouldn't have let me fumble. Entirely gracious and extremely grounded, when I teasingly referred to what she's built as an empire, she quickly corrected me and said she preferred "accomplishment" to "empire."

I reminded her that we'd actually met, or at least stood side by side, when Arlene Blackburn took me to the Tiara Parade at IQF 2004, when dozens of quilters—most who only know each other online—meet in front of Karey's convention center office, sporting ridiculous tiaras, to put faces to their online quilting pals, to vie for first place in the contest, and then to parade down the escalator and through the convention center and out the door down the street to a Chinese restaurant. Not surprisingly, given the joyful chaos of that event—plus, just maybe, the fact that she meets about fifty thousand people at each IQF—Karey laughingly admitted having no recollection whatsoever of this encounter. That didn't stop her from talking to me like an old friend not five minutes into our conversation.

Karey's personal foray into quilting began just before she married in 1963, when she gathered with the women in her family for a bee. Then an unsuccessful bid for a seat in the Texas Legislature in 1974 accidentally pushed her further down the quilting path than she ever might have dreamed of, when she endeavored to pay off her campaign debts by opening up an antique shop that turned into a quilt shop.

Now she has headed up IQF for over thirty years, with no plans for retiring. Business has grown and expanded to include annual shows in Chicago and biannual shows in Europe. Karey works together with a dedicated staff, among them her first cousin, Nancy O'Bryant Puentes, with whom she has published two books that document the history of Texas quilts, quilts they discovered when they set out, over seven years, all across Texas to uncover countless gorgeous quilts that had been passed down through generations. Some of these quilts were also chosen to be featured in an exhibit at the state capitol.

Here, Karey talks about more than three decades of full immersion in the world of quilts, from what motivates her to her thoughts on the quilt police:

" If somebody wants to make sure I'll do something, they'll tell me no. It's sort of like waving a red flag in front of a bull. Tell me something can't be done—I will figure out a way to do it.

I can remember when Nancy and I had decided to do the Texas Quilt Search, and we were told by people all over the United States that that was the biggest waste of time they'd ever heard of, there were no good quilts in Texas and everybody knew that we didn't have any good quilts, and the conditions had been so bad that there simply could not be any good quilts, and why were we doing this?

We decided that wasn't true, and we headed out on a seven-year search and we did indeed find fabulous quilts. In that last couple of years we were gone almost every weekend to somewhere to do a quilt search. This was before 1986—definitely pre-Internet. We worked in each instance with a group in the town—either the guild or the art museum or the history museum or the heritage society—who helped us, who thought this was a really good thing to do in their community, and they got the word out for us. We provided them with news releases, but there were no paid ads.

We photographed the ones that were the most interesting. It was quick, on the spot, not well lit, just done to document the quilts. I did the dating, and the people told us their stories, and this was all taken down by scribes. We had a jury of three people, very well known, who then selected, out of all the slides, the quilts that were in the first part of the exhibit. This was specifically to show for the Texas sesquicentennial that the women of Texas had a large role to play in the civilization of the state and the quilts were reflective of that role.

Reflecting on her memorable achievements:

" I would say one of our most moving moments would be when we did the September 11 quilts. And the other one would be when we did the "20th Century's 100 Best American Quilts." Those two were major, major accomplishments that would rank right up there with the Texas Quilt Search. It's kind of hard to say the September 11 quilts were an accomplishment—using that phrase there is not good. It's like you're capitalizing on a tragedy, which is not at all what we did.

As far as challenges, it was a huge challenge when we had to leave the Sham-

Karey Bresenhan, president of Quilts, Inc., parent company of the International Quilt Festival/Houston, Patchwork and Quilt Expo, International Quilt Festival/Chicago, and the International Quilt Market. Photo courtesy of Quilts, Inc.

rock Hotel and move to a convention center. That nearly did me in because of the expenses that were involved. It looked like every time I turned around, there was some expense that blew me away for something I never had to pay for before. I knew I could make it happen. I knew I would make it happen.

There was one night when I went home and asked my husband, "If I sign this contract, could they take my house?" And he said, "No, Texas is a homestead state. They can't take your house." I said, "Can they take the dog?" He said, "No, Texas is a homestead state. You're entitled to your livestock. The dog counts as livestock." I said, "They can't take the dog and they can't take the house?" He said, "That's right." And I said, "Then I'll sign the contract."

Every time you open a show you go, "Good grief! How did this happen?

How in the world did this happen?" And you think back and you realize how it happened. It happened with an awful lot of hard work from you and a lot of other people. And a lot of good luck. I've always had good luck—please, Lord, don't let it go away.

I also think you make your own luck to a degree. There are things that happen that you didn't really have any control over that opened doors for you and opportunities for you, and what you have to be is ready to see them and ready to take action and take the risk. I've always been a risk taker.

On how she lost the election in 1974 and decided to open an antique shop to repay her campaign debts:

"My mother said, the night I lost [the election], "Oh baby, thank heavens. Now you don't have to go up there and be a crook like all the rest of them!" This is from a woman who had worked like a dog to get me elected. Deep in her heart she was afraid I'd go up there and be a crook like all the rest of the politicians.

The shop came before the show. It came to pay off my political debts from not having won the election. I didn't know that you were supposed to get your political debts forgiven. I paid them all back. But then, they were debts like Mama's retired friend whom she taught kindergarten with, who loaned me the proceeds of her fall wheat crop, and you know she had to have it back because that's what she lived on.

My mother-in-law and I opened the store. For two years I never bought a thing. I never went in a store. I made all the gifts I had to give by hand from whatever I had. But I paid back all those debts. In the shop, we hung my family quilts to hide the places where we didn't have money to put antiques. As the year went on, it seemed like what more and more people really wanted was those quilts. You know, Howard Hughes didn't have enough money to buy a family quilt from me—I wouldn't have sold it. You just didn't sell a family quilt. So I began to make contact with other sources of quilts, and the next thing you know, the shop simply transmogrified into a quilt store.

We started out with fabrics. My mother brought a lot of her fabrics—she had a huge stash—and we cut them up in little pieces and put them in baggies and sold them for like thirty-five cents from an iron baby bed. That was how we started with fabrics. And the money I got from that, I went and bought some bolts of muslin and some bolts of calico, and we built from there. I have this thing—I don't believe in borrowing money. So anything we do, we save for or we figure out how to make it pay for itself.

Her most memorable personal quilting story:

❝ I've told it so many times my office has forbidden me from telling it. This is what started everything, so I'll go ahead and tell it anyway. I am a fifth-generation Texas quilter. I go back to a German great-great-grandmother who left Germany with nothing and came over to Texas after the flu had decimated her family in Germany. She brought her sons and her daughter, Karoline, for whom I'm named, to Texas, because she had some brothers over here. She and Karoline learned to quilt by lamplight in a tent on the Texas prairie. So I go back a long way with quilts.

My mother married with thirteen quilts—that was the tradition. She married a man whose mother had had two sons, no daughters. And so my Gran Patterson made each of those sons thirteen quilts. So quilts were a huge part of my childhood memories. You know, a blue norther blows in, and Mama creeps in and puts a quilt on me that's so heavy you can't turn over under it. And I still have some of those quilts. I love them.

Nancy and I, when she'd spend the night, the next morning the mothers wouldn't let us get up, because they wanted to sleep late. So we'd play paper

---

The love came from my maternal grandmother. I love to collect fabric and will travel any distance for the sale of it. Three yards is my standard purchase, just in case I really like it.

The biggest quilting mistake that I ever made was forgetting to reset my stitch length for basting back to 2.5 or 2.0. I sewed fifty-four log cabin blocks that way before discovering it.

My most satisfying moments of quilting were teaching my fourth graders to piece blocks on various sewing machines. They made Christmas stockings, vests. and pincushions. The smiles on their faces said it all.

—Rhonda Lawton, Plum Creek, Texas

dolls in the nooks and crannies you could make in the quilt—you know, you can make hills and valleys.

The main thing was, when I got married, which was in 1963, my grandmother pulled out a quilt top that I had never seen before and Mama had never seen before. And it seemed that my great-grandmother had made this quilt top when I was born, and it was to be my wedding quilt. Now my great-grandmother had been dead for many years at that point, but Granny had kept the quilt top.

So Granny called in all my great-aunts, all her sisters, to San Antonio, and Mother and Aunt Helen came in from Houston, and Nancy and I came down from the University at Austin, and we quilted that quilt top in one weekend in a family quilting bee that went on to all hours in the night. We ate breakfast, lunch, and dinner out of a huge pot of stew. We slept in what we called Methodist pallets on the floor, which were piles of quilts on the floor. It's an absolutely wonderful memory.

I can remember Granny sitting Nancy and me down at the head of the quilt, and she said, "Now, girls . . ."—and whenever Granny said, "Now, girls," in that tone of voice, you paid real close attention—she said, "Now, girls, you learn to take really pretty little stitches because you're going to have to wake up every morning of your life and look at them." And we learned to take real pretty little stitches.

At the very end, it was four a.m. on Monday morning, and I was due back in graduate school for a class at eight in Austin. We were down to the very center of the star. And it was just Granny and my Great-Aunt Minnie and me, and I remember that Great-Aunt Minnie looked over at Granny, and she said, "You know, Ella, that girl's gonna make a right fair quilter."

I felt like I had just had a diamond crown put on my head because in my family the old ones didn't give compliments that often. You really had to earn one. That was real special. My wedding quilt is right here in my house in a place of honor. It periodically goes on a bed, but right now it's in a Plexiglas chest that shows it off.

I have very little time to quilt now, nor do I let myself, because I find quilting very addictive. What I really love is the actual quilting stitch, the actual quilting of the quilt. I'm not really interested in appliqué and I really don't like to piece, but I love to quilt. Quilting is not meant to be work. Quilting is meant to be something you enjoy and you can't wait to get to, and you find it exhilarating and you find it relaxing. I know those are contradictory words, but it is both of those things. You find it makes you feel better about whatever's happened in your life recently. It's a time of peace. If you're going to have to do something you really hate, why in the world do it? Life is too short.

On the negative attention Hollis' quilt garnered, criticism of art quilts in general, and the quilt police:

"I think it's a crock of hoo-rah. We've had Hollis' quilts, and quilts of Hollis' have won blue ribbons before and no one raised Cain about it. The only reason the Cain got raised this time was because the media made an issue of it. I don't have a dog in that fight. I think it was an artificially created brouhaha.

People are intimidated by change. It's just like a rut. People get comfortable driving down that rut. If they have to go veering off across a field, they don't know what's there. They don't know if there are big bumps or a big drop-off. It's intimidation and fear of the unknown. I really truly believe that there is a place for the traditional quilts and will always be a place for the traditional quilts as well as the art quilts. I don't think that we have to say that it's going to be either-or. That is what scares people. Because the art quilts are growing in acknowledgment and growing in importance and winning big prizes, they're afraid that the traditional quilts are going to dwindle. I don't believe this is ever going to happen.

I think the ones who resent the quilt police so strongly are the art quilters. The reason they resent them so strongly—they have good reason to—is because when they submit a quilt to many shows, the shows are judged by the old standards of the quilt police: the stitches per inch and how they bound their edges and how they turned their corners. This has nothing to do with art quilts, and it has no interest at all for the art quilters. They feel that their quilts are unfairly held back or unfairly judged by these standards that really have nothing to do with them.

On the other hand, if you look at the jillions of people making traditional quilts—and by far, people making traditional quilts are the majority—the ones that want to make a beautiful quilt know that if they pick a Double Wedding Ring, they know what it's going to look like; if they pick pretty fabrics, they know what it's going to look like; and if they quilt it beautifully, they know it will be a pretty quilt. They can know exactly how it's going to turn out. There's nothing wrong with that. Look how many gorgeous traditional quilts have come down through our history.

But for those quilts, I think maybe there do have to be some standards for those quilts. I think that's where the concept of the quilt police—which is a phrase I hate, but I know it's accepted—that's where I think the standards by which they judge are applicable to traditional quilts. But I don't think they are applicable to art quilts.

On the culture of quilting and where it's heading:

" One thing I think is happening: the journal quilts are an interesting development, and they have spread very quickly pretty much all over the world. There are people who are working in groups on journal quilts. It's not so much the journal quilts as it is the connecting of the quilts to one's personal life experiences. I think we're going to see more of that—more quilts that are made and identified as being the result of something that has happened in your life or is important to you as a life experience. I think quilts answer a pretty universal urge for people to be remembered. It's something they can leave behind that says, "I was here. I did this. This was my work. Remember me."

I'm the first one who came up with the journal quilt exhibits. I did not invent journal quilts, but what I have loved about them is that they are a very freeing experience. People who have always made traditional quilts, and they

I have done most other crafts and found that I got bored, but with quilting, the learning curve is infinite, as there is always a new technique or untried pattern. Also, it feels like three separate crafts—design (color and pattern), sewing, and quilting.

My mother likes my quilts, but at ninety years of age and having gone through the Depression, she does not understand buying material, cutting it up, and sewing it back together. Every time she sees me working on one, she shakes her head in disbelief. —Shirley A. Brown, Austin, Texas

want to go past that and they're not sure how, and the idea of tackling a big quilt in a way they have not mastered, this makes them very nervous. But the journal quilt—who can get nervous over a piece of paper? And that's how big they are: the size of a piece of paper. You can do anything on a piece of paper. If it doesn't work, what have you lost? You haven't failed; you've just tried.

In many ways, [the culture of quilting] is like an iceberg. There's the tip up there, which is the quilts that one grows up with. Most of the time the quilts that you grow up with are not particularly works of art. They're utility quilts. They're quilts that were made for use on the bed to keep warm. Nowadays everybody has central heat and air; they don't need the quilts to keep them warm. But if you grew up with a grandmother with a sleeping porch in Texas, you needed the quilts.

So the tip of the iceberg is the quilts people remember but don't think of as having any connection to today at all. And then below is this enormous mass of quilters all over the world. They're not really that visible, although in many cases the quilt shows and the museums that have developed, and the museums that are farsighted enough to exhibit quilts as art, have certainly brought this to the world's attention. Organizations like the International Quilt Association and the shows we run in Europe—these things really have developed a quilting audience where it never existed before.

On how the European shows got started:

“ Mary Penders was a quilting teacher in Virginia. She taught many wives of foreign diplomats to quilt. She was invited to go over to Europe and teach their friends when they were transferred back to their countries. She taught many times for us at festival. She kept saying, "Karey, you've got to run a festival in Europe." And I'd say, "Oh no, Mary. I don't have to." She said, "You do have to. They need a festival like this. They need someplace they can get together. All these people from all these different countries, they don't know each other. They're not connected in any way. You need to do this."

Well, of course that got my guilt connected, so I did agree to go with her. We invited Bonnie Leman, and in 1987 we went to several different countries to consider holding a show in those countries. We established that Salzburg, Austria, would be a good place to do this, and once I saw it and once I talked to the people, I realized it's really just a show like any other show. It's just in a different currency. Oh, we're so innocent sometimes . . . [*She laughs.*]

We ran the show and everybody told us we couldn't do that. That was another example of those things you can't do that I went ahead and did. People said, "Europeans will never cooperate"; "You won't have five hundred people who'll attend"; "They will all bad-mouth it because they love to criticize." These were Europeans who were telling me this. I said, "Quilters are different. I think they will come and I don't think they will be that critical, and I think they'll have a good time, and we're going to try it anyway."

And so we did, and we had about twelve hundred people come. I remember at the end I had a meeting with one of the ladies who had been so outspoken about how it would never work. She was an art historian, a very smart young woman from Germany. She said, "I just wanted to tell you I was wrong." I said, "That's okay. I knew you were wrong. It's okay to be wrong." She said, "I don't understand it. We Europeans love to criticize." I said, "I think then it's a good combination because we Americans love to fix things. When people at this show criticized things, we fixed it. And they were always so astonished, but we fixed it right then and there." And she said, "Yes, I know, and they are astonished."

It would be like someone from Spain would come up and say, "Switzerland has two more lights on their quilts than we do. This is not right!" They were prepared to fight. And we would say, "Oh, you're right. That's not right. We'll get you some more lights." About thirty minutes later we'd give them their two lights. And it was just great, because they couldn't understand they were getting what they asked for without having to argue with us.

Now I can go almost anywhere in Europe and someone will come up to me, very shy and tentative, and say, "You're the quilt lady." And I'll say, "Yes, ma'am, I am." And they'll say, "I was at Salzburg"—not any of the other cities, but Salzburg. That was a very special thing we did, that first one. When we had the roll call of the nations at that first event, that was really something to see. Everybody in that room was excited and thrilled that they were part of something that was bigger than them. You could walk out in little sidewalk cafés everywhere, and you knew they were quilters because they couldn't speak each other's language but they were talking with their hands. And you could stand there and tell what they were talking about.

On looking back over the thirty years:

"It's been a great, wild, wonderful ride, I can tell you that. It's been extremely hard work, many, many, many long hours. Gorgeous, gorgeous quilts. I have been so fortunate to see so many fabulous quilts and to see them as they surfaced. To see Katie Pasquini's art quilt win Best of Show in one of our shows in Houston—I think that might've been the first art quilt to win a Best of Show. Of course from that so many different things have sprung up. To see the way machine quilting has changed—and really changed the way people see quilts today.

I was one of the last holdouts. Nancy and I were. We were very strongly against machine quilting. And about ten years ago we finally actually took our blinders off and looked at what was being done and said, "Good Lord, when did this start happening?" and realized we were basically being old-fashioned and not keeping up with the times.

We removed our objection, and machine quilting began being accepted in Houston at that point. I have to tell you I think the quality and amount of machine quilting that is being done on quilts today has actually changed people's perception of how a quilt should be quilted. When you stand today and look at a beautiful hand-quilted quilt, and maybe it's hanging next to a beautiful machine-quilted quilt, the hand-quilted quilt almost looks like it needs more quilting. It doesn't really need more quilting, but your eye is now more accustomed to seeing the vast amount of stitching and the closeness of the stitching of the machine-quilted quilt. And so when you look at the hand-quilted quilt, your brain thinks, "That needs more quilting." I think that's an interesting side effect of machine quilting.

Quilting is so relaxing. I love fabric. I love shopping for, touching, combining the fabrics. I love taking a pattern—wearable or flat piece—and changing it to make it my own. I love the people in quilting and attending various quilt events. I love giving my quilts away and watching the faces of the receivers light up. But most of all, I love watching them change and grow on my design wall as I progress through a project.

—Dana Stieferman, Round Rock, Texas

19

Binding

I believe in supernatural occurrences. Many of my friends lovingly pooh-pooh this belief system of mine and point out that what I claim to be unusual occurrences are simply common coincidences. I can't make them believe me, but as an atheist friend of mine told me, recounting a conversation with a priest friend of his, the priest said, "I don't need you to believe. I just need you to believe that I believe."

Over the course of piecing this book together from the fabric of a vast stash of amazing quilters, I continuously encountered people who knew about quilting. And I met some of them in odd settings. I met them often without even trying. As I've noted, this in itself is not probably a major supernatural phenomenon. Quilters are everywhere.

But I did have a couple of notable experiences where I had to laugh at my great fortune at having some invisible hand lift me up and drop me straight into the lap of a great quilting connection. The first of these experiences happened in my own living room. I had invited a few friends over for dinner. As we were sitting and chatting, I mentioned that I was working on a book about quilting. My friend Laura Freeman, who is a children's entertainer, sat up straight in the rocking chair and immediately belted out the opening lines to some song about how this piece of fabric (Laura held up an imaginary piece of fabric) was once a piece of her wedding dress.

Laura then went on to recount how, years before, she'd lived in Johnson City, Texas, where she'd moved to join her old high school choir director in helping bring to the small stage there a production of a Broadway musical called *The Quilters*. I was pretty surprised that I'd never heard of this musical, but I delighted when Laura arranged for us to drive out to Johnson City and watch a videotape of the show in the home of a woman named Joy, who had been a cast member.

Here I have a confession to make. You'd've thought by this point—I was close to finishing the book—that I would have known, from having met such a diverse group of quilters from all backgrounds and of many different life philosophies, not to prejudge this musical. But I confess, on the drive to Johnson City, that I fully expected to see something schmaltzy. I certainly didn't count on any envelopes being pushed.

In 1965 my grandmother came for a visit, and she always like to stay busy, so my father bought some cross-stitch quilt blocks to embroider. My grandmother, mother, sister, and I—and even my father (who had taught me how to embroider)—all worked on the blocks. We finished them, and they got put away. Then in 1971 my father was diagnosed with cancer, and my mother got the blocks out to work on the quilt for therapy, and also because she knew it would please my father to have it finished.

She set the blocks and put on the border, started hand-quilting it, and then my father passed away. It was hard for her to work on it, so she put it away. Years later she got it out again, but when her eyesight started getting so bad from macular degeneration that she couldn't work on it anymore, she put it away again. In the mid-eighties she got it out and asked that I finish quilting it, so I did.

In 2000 that quilt hung in the Austin Area Quilt Show in the multigenerational category. My mother came to see it, and we stood there looking at that finished quilt, thinking of how many hours we had all spent making it. And it made it seem as though my father and grandmother, who were no longer with us, were standing there with us looking at it with pride.

—Janis Keene, Round Rock, Texas

After driving down a long private road, we arrived at a large log cabin in a clearing. Before knocking on the door, we stopped to pet the donkeys in the yard, one of which was slated for a starring role that night in a nearby living Nativity scene being put on at a local church by Joy's sister. As we patted the donkeys, Joy came up behind us, grinning and handing us Nilla Wafers to feed to the beasts. Her sweatshirt beamed the word "JOY!" Inside the cabin, there was a Christmas tree in every room.

We popped the tape in and settled in to watch. Laura explained that each vignette was based on a true story of a real quilter. If ever the *Vagina Monologues* had a predecessor, this was it. The musical tackled topics like bad husbands, dreaded spinsterhood, first periods, infant mortality, illegal abortions, and more. In essence, it was a string of real stories, often about wrenching events many women throughout history have faced and often still face. To imagine this work—which was downright radical in certain scenes—presented in a small Texas town impressed me.

About a month after this happened, I was teaching an after-school writing club at my son's middle school. That day, a student named Zeke was in attendance. I've known Zeke since he was a tiny baby—I write for the newspaper his father owns. I was surprised to see him at the club, as he isn't a member. But that day, his regular program was canceled, so he came to join me while he waited for a ride home. I assigned the kids a writing exercise and then sat down at a nearby computer to send off an e-mail I'd forgotten to send earlier in the day.

The note I sent was a request to Louis Black, the editor of the *Austin Chronicle*, which Zeke's dad, Nick Barbaro, owns. Louis is one of the most connected guys in Austin. I had been so caught up in quilts, I decided it was time to take the next step and make a documentary on the topic. So I sent Louis a note asking for fundraising ideas.

Louis wrote back immediately to inform me that Nick's Aunt Norma had cowritten the book *The Quilters*, upon with the musical had been based—yes, the very same musical I'd just watched a performance of in Joy's living room. If that weren't amazing enough, as I was reading this, Zeke's mom, Susan, walked into the room. I steered her out into the hallway. Was it really true her aunt-in-law had written *The Quilters*?

Susan laughed. Not only was it true, but Susan had recently vacationed with Aunt Norma and was certain the two of us would really hit it off. She put us in touch the next day. Which is how I came to be friends with Norma Bradley Allen. I e-mailed her, and she responded right away, launching into tales about the book and about the days when she knew Karey Bresenhan and spoke at an early quilt festival. Just as I was pleased, when interviewing Karey, that I understood the things she was talking about, it was very amazing, and amusing, to me that here I was, on the tail end of finishing this book, and meeting another woman who'd written a book featuring the tales of quilters.

Not only that, but Norma let me in on a little secret. She's never made a quilt. This consoled me. Because as I sit here, I confess that I have still not quilted my first first quilt. It is sitting, pinned and ready to go, in a basket under my sewing table. On the other hand, I'm no longer afraid of that quilt. For now, my problem getting it done is just a total lack of time. Which, I think, makes me more of a quilter than not. How I wish I had eight or ten hours to sit and knock that thing out.

But I still have the two tiny quilts I made to hold me over and give me the rights to say, with a semi-straight face, I have conquered my goal. *I have quilted.* But not until that first first quilt is spread across my bed will I send out gold-engraved notes declaring triumph.

In the meanwhile, I remain entirely bowled over by the quilters I've met— either in person or through their surveys—in the past few years. Until Sarah clued me into this vast world, I didn't have the faintest hint of its existence. Now, I'm happy to say, people call me and e-mail and stop me all the time to tell me this or that thing they heard about quilting. Quilting has become as much a part of my life as it is for those of you who actually quilt on a regular basis.

I'm going to stop typing now. And I swear, I am going to dedicate the time I once spent typing up transcripts of conversations with quilters to sitting down at that old thrift-shop sewing machine and finishing up that *first* first quilt of mine. At which point I plan to launch right into my second quilt. Surely Mrs. Haggard, my old eighth-grade home-ec teacher, will roll over in her grave once I start.

Epilogue

Books, like quilts, sometimes take longer to finish than originally intended. I figure I started writing this book in 2004, earlier if you count the unintentional research I did when Sarah first took me to the 2002 International Quilt Fest. I thought I'd pretty well finished writing it on New Year's Eve, 2004. I was staying with some friends in Real de Catorce, a little Mexican village in the Sierra Mountains. Folks there have a very big, very loud celebration, and being terrified of fireworks, I used the excuse of needing to finish writing as a reason to avoid the festivities. As the clock struck midnight, I ushered in 2005 with a grin and a sigh. The book (I thought) was finished.

Well, what do you know? It's now almost a full year later. Turns out the book needed tweaking, which required input from editors and readers, which took time. Now here I am—maybe coincidence, maybe fate—back in Mexico for another New Year's celebration. In the twelve months that have passed, I managed to finish that first first quilt of mine, which I display proudly on my bed and admire daily. Really, I cannot believe I put all those little pieces together.

More than the satisfaction I get from having completed a real quilt, I realize that all these years of hanging around with quilters has changed me for the better. I feel like I've attended some full-immersion language school and now I don't have to stop and translate every little term someone uses. Better still, I feel like I've been infected by the generosity and good nature of the many quilters I've met.

This came in handy in the fall of 2005. I teach part-time at a very small private high school. In September one of our students, Austin, was hit by a truck and died. This would be devastating under any circumstances and in any community. But because we are such a small group, it hit especially hard.

The day after Austin died, we all gathered in the school theater. In forty-two years, never have I heard or seen or felt such collected grief. We were overcome, barely able to speak. We sat and bawled our eyes out. From time to time, one or another of us tried to offer a few consoling words to the others. Without thinking, as if in a total trance, I stood up and heard myself announce to the room that I would be spearheading an art project for Austin's mom, that we could probably make a quilt together.

Had I really said that?

Indeed.

Still in shock and weighed down by sorrow, I went to the fabric store and bought a couple of yards of white quilting fabric, some acrylic paints, and fabric markers. I brought them to school, and the students and teachers made dozens of squares. Then my friend Kayci, who owns a boutique and who

---

Quilting reminds me of my roots. It tells me to be humble and frugal. But a good by-product is that is relieves a lot of stress.

When I was in third grade, my mother and her friends were making a quilt for my aunt. I was sitting under the quilt frame watching the ladies hands work the fabric. I could see the sun shine through the stitches. When one of the ladies went home, mom said that she needed my help. I told her that I was too little and my stitches were ugly. She said that did not matter. To this day, those ugly stitches are still there. Secure. I have learned that as long as a child did it, there is magic in it. —Monica Price, Austin, Texas

makes a lot of clothing featuring iron-on transfers, took some photos of Austin and made them into transfers, which she ironed onto more squares. I contemplated the pile of finished squares for some time. What had I gotten myself into? Despite having made two tiny quilts and that one lap quilt, I hardly felt like I knew what I was doing. But I had set a goal, and there was no turning back.

I invited two of my students, Bonnie and Blossom, to assist me in assembling the quilt. They came to my house several days, and thankfully both knew how to operate a sewing machine. (Bonnie even taught me the right way to put in pins.) Over many hours the girls cut out printed fabric squares to alternate with the painted squares, came up with a layout, and then sewed and sewed.

Originally I had hoped we would finish by Thanksgiving, but the best-laid plans of writers and quilters often go astray. Instead we finished it right before Christmas. The closer we got to finishing, the more overwhelmed I started to feel. I knew going into the project that this quilt would mean a lot to Austin's mom, Holly. But as Bonnie and Blossom put their energy into it, and as I looked at the photo squares of Austin and the painted squares with messages from those who loved and missed him so much, I began to really feel, for the first time, the incredible power a single quilt can wield.

I called Holly and asked if we could come by with a gift. I warned her that it might be very emotional and told her we could wait until the holidays had passed if that would be easier. She said no, it was fine to come over sooner rather than later.

Three days before Christmas, as Bonnie and Blossom and I drove to Holly's, I confess I worried. What would she say? What would we say? How would she receive it?

Holly greeted us warmly, and we sat at her kitchen table. She unwrapped the box slowly, stopping to tell stories about Austin. Finally, the paper was off and she lifted the lid. I have been writing since before I was eight—well over thirty years—and yet I will never be able to capture in words the look on her face or the feeling in that room when Holly pulled our little quilt out and held it up and realized what it was made of. Tears filled her eyes, and she clutched it tightly. "I never knew anything like this could exist," she said. I choked back my own tears.

This is what the quilting community has brought me. I understand now the power of the quilt. The creative outlet. The ability to infuse "mere" cloth with deep sentiment. What a world Sarah opened for me. What comfort I have found there.

One other thing happened as a result of that memorial quilt. As Bonnie and Blossom and I worked on it, Blossom's widower father, Herman, tuned in to the fact that his daughter was spending a lot of time with me. We got to talking up at the school one night after a student art show.

A month later, Herman asked me out for coffee. Four months after that, we got married. Our bed, not surprisingly, is covered in quilts—one an Around-the-World pattern made for me by Sarah, who took me to my first show, and the other a quilt my friend Shaun gave me, made by his grandmother, the classic Wedding Band design.